Life

Brandon Park
With Josh Hunt

All Scripture references English Standard Version unless otherwise noted.

Table of Contents

Special Thanks

Special thanks to Denette Hales and Kellie Sharpe   for help with this book.

Foreword

Godly saints live with eternity in mind. They live with a daily awareness that this world is not our home, we are just passing through. They are sold out to the cause of glorifying God by doing all they can to get people out of Hell and into Heaven.

Pulpits today say too little of Heaven and Hell. Preachers are too cautious to offend. We can't get people out of Hell and into Heaven by ignoring the subject.

The great revivals were fueled, in part, with sermons on Heaven and Hell. The classic example, or course, is Jonathan Edwards' sermon, *Sinners in the Hands of an Angry God.* Although that tone may not be appropriate to today's world, the message is timeless.

Brandon Park is one of the God-anointed preachers of the next generation. He fills his pulpit each Sunday with solid biblical sermons on fire with the Holy Spirit.

This book is about an important topic: what happens after this life is over. It is solidly biblical and communicated with compassion, conviction and clarity.

Dr. Johnny Hunt,
Senior Pastor
First Baptist Church of Woodstock, Georgia

CHAPTER 1
Facing the Fear of Death

"Yea, though I walk through the valley of the shadow of death, I will fear no evil: for thou art with me."
- Psalm 23:4

There will come a time when the only thing you can think about is death. Perhaps when you are standing over her casket. It won't matter whether you have the latest iPhone. It won't matter what shape your bank account is in. It won't matter whether you bought that car or not, or whether you have gained or lost a few pounds. All you will be able to think about is death.

Death. We push the thought out of our minds most of the time. At least, I do. It is not a happy thing to think about. It is so creepy I try to avoid it at all costs.

As a pastor, I do a lot of funerals and have to think about it more than most. As a pastor, it is my job to help prepare you for it. That is what this book is about.

I'll never forget going to my first funeral service. I was just a six-year-old kid. Our neighbor, Mr. Knight had died and as a family we were doing our neighborly duty in attending the service. Yet even to this day, I remember the feeling of seeing a dead body for the first time. The man I once knew as being so friendly and loving and offering me those delicious orange colored, marshmallow-like **Circus Peanuts** was now lying down like a frozen statue in a wooden box. It was so disturbing. I felt I had to get out of there. I lied and told my Mom that I was sick and needed to go to the van—I think I would have said anything at that moment just to be able to leave. That was my first experience with coming face to face with the reality of death. Creepy, disturbing and totally freaked me out!

However, in my line of work, I've done more funerals than I would care to imagine. I've seen it all. Some families mourn and sob uncontrollably with grief as they say goodbye to their loved ones before the casket is closed. Others give them a kiss on the cheek, a pat on the shoulder, as if to say, "I'll see you tomorrow." We all process grief differently. With some, you can almost sense their fear and apprehension with death, as they don't even want to be close to or touch the casket.

When I preached the series of sermons on which this book is based, we had a casket on the stage as I preached. It freaked some people out.

Isn't it interesting how an inanimate object, like a wooden box, can make us feel so uncomfortable? My goal in writing this book is that your fear of the afterlife will melt away as you learn the truth of what awaits all of us when we are in right relationship with God.

The fact of the matter is, all of us will die.

I'd like to share with you two dates that are very important to me. The first date is September 17th, 1981. The reason that date is so very important to me is because that is the date of my birth.

Allow me to give you another date that's at least mildly amusing to me—it's the date of October 20, 2069. Now why is that date so interesting? In researching for this book, I came across a very interesting website called www.Death-Clock.org. On that website, they ask you for your date of birth and you answer a few questions about your health and BMI (Body Mass Index). Based on that information, the site will give you an estimated date of your expiration.

I was interested to find out that this website says my last day on earth is estimated to be October 20th 2069 and that I'll live to be 88 years 1 month and 3 days. That means that at the time of this writing, I supposedly only have 20,623 days left to live.

Now obviously, I don't believe in the accuracy or the validity of the Death-Clock.org site. Yet it does illustrate the fact that God does have a death-clock for you and for me. That clock is ticking for every one of us. The Bible says, "*Teach us to number our days that we may get a heart of wisdom*." Psalm 90:12

You can't really get away from death. Have you ever noticed how much of our news on TV centers around death and dying? It is estimated that about 75% of what we see on the news is somehow related to death in one way or another.

We don't typically have the feeling of the fear of death unless we have encountered the close call of an accident, or if we are sitting at the bedside of a loved one whose time on this earth is coming to a close. We certainly feel the fear of death if we receive that "bad news" from our doctor.

Back in 2010, I came face-to-face with my own mortality. I went to the doctor for a complete physical because I had been sick for so long and I wasn't making any improvement. The doctor told me I was facing a possible diagnosis of lymphoma—a cancer of the lymph glands. I faced a full battery of tests in the days ahead and I remember that feeling of lying awake at night, not knowing if I would be here five years from now. The day that I was to receive my final CAT Scan results I stayed home from work, paced the floor, and waited for the phone to ring. Finally, that call I was expecting came through, "Your CAT Scan shows no evidence of cancer." What a relief. I felt like I had dodged a bullet. But the lessons that I learned during that season of waiting taught me a lot about what it means to walk with God when the future of your life existence seems so uncertain.

It's unfortunate that most people don't start giving much thought to their life's end until their sunset years. A New York professor of gerontology said "It's not until midlife before people really become aware of their mortality." Young people seldom, if ever, think about death.

It's been said that death is the subject that we spend a lifetime trying not to think about. Yet the imminence and reality of death is all around us.

Maybe you're like me. Perhaps you've often wondered, "What is it going to be like when I die?" Let's examine God's Word to find those answers together.

My prayer for you is that when the time comes for your life to end, that there will be more joy than there will be fear. **We do have to face death, but we don't have to fear death**. Because the Bible says in Hebrews 2:15 that Jesus came to "*Deliver those who have lived all their lives as slaves to the fear of dying.*" (NLT)

We Will Fear Death
If We Face It Unknown

Why is it so important to study the afterlife? The answer is very simple. **What you believe about death and eternity will determine how you live.**

There are a lot of people who have a lot of misconceptions about death.

Atheists believe that once you die, it's over. There is no eternity. You're worm dirt. You're pushing up daisies, and there's no reason to live with an eternal motivation.

Others believe in a place called purgatory—a holding cell where a person stays until God can figure out what to do with you. Catholics believe that after death, some people will go to purgatory. Their loved ones can pray for them so they can leave purgatory. However, the Bible's teaching on the subject of purgatory is non-existent.

Islam teaches that at the end, Allah will judge your works. If your good works outweigh your bad you'll go to paradise. If your bad works outweigh your good, you'll go to Hell.

Hindus and some New Agers believe in reincarnation. They think that if you've been really good, you'll come back in a higher life form. If you've been really bad, you'll come back as a lower life form—a cockroach or a mosquito.

What you believe about death and eternity will determine how you live.

The Bible teaches that when we die we will face judgment and we will exist for all eternity in one of two destinations: Heaven or Hell. We don't go to Heaven based on works. Rather, the Bible teaches, **"by grace you have been saved by faith."** (Ephesians 2.8) If you are eager to find out more, skip to the last chapter.

The main reason why people, even Christians, fear death is because it is unknown to them. The truth of the matter is, "Ignorance is a breeding ground for fear."

Let me illustrate by asking a question. Did you have a hard time sleeping last night because you were worried about monsters underneath your bed? Chances are you probably didn't. We know *about* monsters (they are scary) but we also know the *truth* about monsters (they don't exist), which cancels out our fear. My three small children know about monsters—but they still don't know the truth about monsters (at least they're not totally convinced they're not real) and because of that—they fear. Their fear is unwarranted.

The same principle is true about Christians when it comes to the fear of death. It's amazing how many Christians have the wrong beliefs about death and the afterlife. And because of their ignorance—it becomes a breeding ground for fear. **You don't have to be afraid of death when you understand the promises of God.** The Bible says, "*To be absent from the body is to be at home with the Lord*." (2 Corinthians 5:8)

Let's examine the teaching of Scripture for what we know about death.[1]

Death is an inevitable certainty

The studies are conclusive. George Bernard Shaw said, "The statistics on death are quite impressive. One out of one people die."

Unless you are a believer and Jesus returns in your lifetime—you are going to die.

Hebrews 9:27 says, "*And just as it is appointed for man to die once, and after that comes judgment*."

The word translated **appointed** could literally be translated **reserved.** God has made a reservation for your death. When you make a reservation at a hotel that means that a certain room has been set aside for your use. Every one of us has a reservation with death and it is one reservation that you cannot cancel.

People keep this appointment every day. The numbers of people that enter into eternity are staggering.

- 3 people every second

- 180 people every minute

- 11,000 people every hour

- 260,000 people ever day

- 95,000,000 people every year

What happens at your judgment depends on what you did with Jesus Christ during your lifetime. Yes, we are going to die—but something makes us live and think as if we won't.

Perhaps it's even one of the enemy's greatest tactics—to allow our minds to be so distracted that we don't give any thought to what life will be like in the world to come. That was Satan's strategy in the Garden of Eden. In the book of Genesis, the serpent (Satan) said to Eve regarding the eating of the forbidden fruit, "**You shall not die.**" (Genesis 3:4) Satan contradicted what God had said. God said to Adam that if they were to eat of that fruit, they would surely die. The devil said, "**You will not die**" and he has been telling people this ever since.

Today, people live and act as if they were going to live forever—giving no thought to the fact that someday sooner or later, their life is going to come to an end. However, that doesn't change the fact that we will all die.

Death is not the end of life, but a transition to a different life

I want you to imagine a scenario. Picture twin babies inside a mother's womb. One asks the other, "Do you believe in life after delivery?"

The other replies, "Why, of course, there has to be something after delivery. Maybe we are here to prepare ourselves for what we will be later."

You don't have to be afraid of death when you understand the promises of God.

"Nonsense," says the other. "There is no life after delivery. What would that life be?"

"I don't know but there will be more light than here. Maybe we will walk with our legs and eat from our mouths."

The other says, "That is absurd! Walking is impossible. And eat with our mouths? Ridiculous. The umbilical cord supplies nutrition. Life after delivery is to be excluded. The umbilical cord is too short."

"I think there is something and maybe it's different than it is here," the other replies.

"No one has ever come back from there. Delivery is the end of life, and in the after-delivery, it is nothing but darkness and it takes us nowhere."

"Well, I don't know," says the other twin, "but certainly we will see mother and she will take care of us."

"Mother? You believe in mother? Where is she now?"

"She's all around us! It's in here that we live. Without her there would not be this world."

"I don't see her, so it's only logical to reason that she doesn't exist."

"Sometimes when you're in silence you can hear her, you can perceive her. I believe there is a reality after delivery and we're to prepare ourselves for that reality."

After the first nine months of our existence, life doesn't cease to exist. No, life is just beginning. It's taking on a whole other form. There would be no way to explain to a pre-born child the amazing grandeur of the world or the sensations they will experience—it's far greater than their ability to sense or imagine it. And so it will be in eternity. Death is not a period to our existence, it is a comma. We transition into a different life where we will be more alive and more aware than we are right now.

Immediately after death four things happen:

1. At the moment of death, the conscious-ness of our soul is immediately awakened.

You may be in a coma or you may pass away in your sleep – but in that moment of death, we will instantly be aware of what is happening. We will *immediately* be in the presence of God or we will be separated from God. There is absolutely no mention of purgatory or "soul sleep" in the Bible.

In 2 Corinthians 5:8, Paul said that, "*to be absent from the body is to be at home with the Lord.*" At that precise moment of death, those who are in Christ will be ush-ered into the presence of God.

2. There is an initial separation of the soul from the body

At the exact moment of death, the soul and the body separate. The real "you" is not your body. I may have skin and real flesh but what you see of Brandon Park is not the real me. In the Bible, your present body is called a "tent"—it is just a temporary outer covering—while our future body is referred to as a "*building from God, a house not made with hands, eternal in the Heavens.*" (2 Corinthians 5:1)

So this body, or tent, is a house for the real you but it's not really you. At the moment of death, your body dies but you will continue to live.

Jesus said, "*And do not fear those who kill the body but cannot kill the soul. Rather fear him who can destroy both soul and body in Hell.*" Matthew 10:28

When your physical body dies, you will be just as alive as you have ever been. Someone will be making preparations for your memorial service. Someone else will be making potato salad for the reception—but you will still be very much alive.

At that very moment, there will either be immense joy or there will be intense horror when our soul leaves our body.

You see, right now, we are all covered under what theologians call "common grace." It doesn't matter if you are a Christian or not—when it rains, it doesn't just rain on the yards of those who are only Christians—it rains on everybody's yard!

God offers to this world a common grace that's available to all. But at the point of death, there's either going to be absolute grace (in fullness of measure in ways we can't even imagine) or there will be absolute total absence of grace as you are eternally separated from God.

3. There is a future resurrection of the body
1 Thessalonians 4:13-18 says,

But we do not want you to be uninformed, brothers, about those who are asleep, that you may not grieve as others do who have no hope. For since we believe that Jesus died and rose again, even so, through Jesus, God will bring with him those who have fallen asleep. For this we declare to you by a word from the Lord, that we who are alive, who are left until the coming of the Lord, will not precede those who have fallen asleep. For the Lord himself will descend from Heaven with a cry of command, with the voice of an archangel, and with the sound of the trumpet of God. And the dead in Christ will rise first. Then we who are alive, who are left, will be caught up together with them in the clouds to meet the Lord in the air, and so we will always be with the Lord. Therefore encourage one another with these words.

So the Bible teaches that someday at the resurrection we're going to have a physical body that will be assigned to our soul. Regardless of whether a person is headed for the New Heaven and New Earth or the Lake of Fire in Hell—we are all going to receive a new body.

The question is often asked, "What about cremation? Is it acceptable for a Christian to be cremated or is burial the only solution for our body after we're done with it?" There is no teaching in the Bible specifically about cremation. Nothing in Scripture forbids it. We do understand that there is a historical precedence of burial in Scripture. Most of the key people in the Old Testament were buried, but that doesn't mean it's the only way. There are Christians who object to the practice of cremation. Their arguments are based on the Biblical concept that one day the bodies of those who have died in Christ will be resurrected and reunited with their souls—so if a body has been destroyed by fire, it's impossible for it to be resurrected later.

Whether you're cremated or buried—we are all going to end up as dust eventually. Whether or not you choose cremation for yourself or your loved ones is a personal decision that will not affect your personal destiny.

4. There is a final judgment and consignment of the body with the soul

Jesus said:

> *When the Son of Man comes in his*
> *glory, and all the angels with him,*
> *then he will sit on his glorious throne.*
> *Before him will be gathered all the*
> *nations, and he will separate people*
> *one from another as a shepherd*
> *separates the sheep from the goats.*
> *And he will place the sheep on his*
> *right, but the goats on the left. Then*

the King will say to those on his right,
'Come, you who are blessed by my
Father, inherit the kingdom prepared
for you from the foundation of the
world. Matthew 25:31–34

For the Christian, the final judgment will be when rewards will be given. We'll discuss this more in the chapter on rewards. After we receive our rewards, we will be so overcome with gratitude and the grace that God has provided that we will give them back to the Lord Jesus Christ by laying them down at His feet in an act of worship.

As a believer, death should be viewed as the ideal

Paul said:

For to me to live is Christ, and to die is gain. If I am to live in the flesh, that means fruitful labor for me. Yet which I shall choose I cannot tell. I am hard pressed between the two. My desire is to depart and be with Christ,

> *When your physical body dies, you will be just as alive as you have ever been.*

15

for that is far better. But to remain
in the flesh is more necessary on your
account. Philippians 1:21–24

Paul knew he could go right back into Jerusalem and start preaching and he would be stoned to death. But, because people still needed him to fulfill his mission, he stayed the course. Paul longed for that day when God would call him home through his death.

Death is the door to eternal life. A girl took a short-cut through the cemetery and her friends asked her why she would do such a thing. She told them it was the shortest way to get her home.[2] The grave surely is the quickest way for us to get to our Heavenly home.

To die young is not to die prematurely

Please don't ever think that if a person dies at a certain age, it's premature.

As we saw earlier, death is not an accident—it is an appointment.

Ecclesiastes 3:1-2 says, "*There is an appointed time for everything. And there is a time for every event under Heaven—a time to give birth and a time to die.*"

God has also said in Psalm 139:16, "*Your eyes have seen my unformed substance; and in Your book were all written the days that were ordained for me, when as yet there was not one of them.*"

Whenever someone dies unexpectedly (especially when they are young), their loved ones are tempted to blame themselves, other people, or God Himself for their premature death. They say things like, "If only this had happened…if only I had done this…if only we didn't go there." The reality is that the number of that person's days were already ordained for him or her before the day they were even born.

A man who was a pilot asked his friend if he wanted to go up in his little Cessna airplane for a ride. "John, you've never been up in an airplane have you?"

John replied, "No sir…never have. I don't have any intention of ever going up in an airplane."

The pilot said, "Come on, John…don't you want to go up and see God's beautiful creation?"

"No, no, no…I'm not going up there."

"John, let me ask you a question…aren't you a Christian?"

"Oh yes sir, I love the Lord with all my heart."

The pilot said, "Well, John don't you believe that as a Christian, when your time comes, your time comes?"

He said, "Oh yes sir…I know that everybody has a time and when my time comes, my time comes!"

The pilot said, "Well John, I don't get it…you're a Christian. You love the Lord. You believe that when your time comes, your time comes—why won't you go fly with me?"

To which John replied, "We may get up there and *your* time may come!"

Sometimes we *say* that we believe in the sovereignty of God, however, we like to insert that word "*but…*" No, God has a perfect plan for every life on this earth and there is no such thing as a premature death.

Heaven is the perfect place to be

A lot of people have the wrong idea of what eternity is going to be like. They imagine it to be like some boring church service with songs they don't like and people they don't know. We're going to see that Heaven is going to be eternal life restored here on this earth. We're going to be able to live like we live now without sin and without pain.

Revelation 21:4 teaches us that "*He will wipe away every tear from their eyes, and death shall be no more, neither shall there be mourning, nor crying, nor pain anymore, for the former things have passed away.*"

A few weeks ago I made myself a cup of coffee. I thought I had put some sugar in my coffee but when I got back up to my office and I tasted it, it was bitter. I just kept on drinking. As I drank more and more of the coffee, it started getting sweeter and sweeter. Until finally when I got to the bottom of the cup, I realized that I had put my sugar in but I had not stirred it up. It would have been a whole lot better if I had stirred the sugar and had enjoyed the sweetness all the way through the coffee.

Through this book, as we study Heaven, I hope to stir up your cup a little bit. I believe that if you are truly saved, God will be there to meet with you and He will give you dying grace when you come to the moment of death. I want you to get hold of the sweetness that will help alleviate the fear of death as you think about it in your daily life.

We Will Fear Death
If We Face It Unatoned

God never prepared Hell for human beings. In Matthew 25:41, Jesus said, "*Then he will say to those on his left, 'Depart from me, you cursed, into the eternal fire prepared for the devil and his angels*.'" Hell wasn't created for man, it was created for Satan and his demons. Mankind goes to Hell when he makes the same decision that Satan and the fallen angels made.

I can hear someone thinking, "I don't know anybody who would deliberately choose and make a decision to go to Hell"—and that's true. If you were to ask people point-blank, "Do you want to spend an eternity in a lake of fire?" The answer would always be, "NO!"

In the same way, a man doesn't rob a bank with the intention of spending the rest of his life in a maximum security prison. But, it is a consequence of his actions.

Hell is a built-in consequence of rejecting Jesus Christ. All a person has to do to choose Hell is to say to Jesus Christ, "I do not want any part of you!"

God has set up so many blockades on the road to Hell. The Bible says in Romans 1 that God has given us the testimony of His creation. A lot of folks have wondered, "What about those who have never had the chance to hear the gospel? What happens to them?"

Romans 1 answers that question for us. It says God has given us the testimony of His creation to lead us to Him. A person can look at this world and look into the stars and know that this creation must be the result of a Creator. If an individual will respond to the light that God has already given to them through the witness of His creation, I believe that God will be sure to send more light. He makes Himself known to those who truly seek Him and seek Truth.

Some people think that we should go to Heaven by default—that somehow we are entitled to live in God's house!

There have been stories of missionaries who have gone into some of the remotest parts of the jungle bringing the gospel and the native people told them, "We have been praying that we would receive the truth. We know there must be a God. We knew that He was a loving God and wants us to know Him. Thank you for telling us His name is Jesus!"

They responded to the truth that they had already been given—and God led them to more Truth, leading to salvation.

And yet here in the God-blessed United States of America—there is a church on every corner, there is preaching on radio and television all the time! For a person to go to Hell from this country—they have to climb over the cross of Jesus Christ to get there!

Man does not go to Hell for what he *does*, but for what he *does not* do—and that is refusing to believe in Jesus Christ and receive His offer of eternal life. Hell is man's default destination.

Perhaps you may have wondered, "How can a loving God send people to hell?"

The short answer is, He doesn't. Men send themselves to Hell by refusing to accept the free gift of eternal life. The Lord is, "*not wishing that any should perish, but that all should reach repentance.*" 2 Peter 3:9

Some people think that we should go to Heaven by default—that somehow we are entitled to live in God's house!

I want you think about it this way—suppose that I found the richest person who lives in my city and he resides in the most beautiful mansion in the entire region. And suppose I pack my house into a U-Haul and I show up at his house with my wife and three small children and say, "Excuse me sir…but we want to live with you! We would like to move into your house."

What do you think he would say to me? He would probably say, "Get lost! I don't know you. You aren't coming into my house!"

Why? <u>Because he doesn't have a relationship with me</u>. In the same way, people who question God's fairness, live their entire lives having nothing to do with God and yet, they expect that when they die they are going to come knocking at God's door and say, "Um…Excuse me, God! I really want to come and live with You now!"

And the Lord will say, "*Depart from me…for I never knew you*" (Matthew 7:23).

Let's turn the tables. If some guy off the street came and knocked on your door and said, "Hey! I've been a good person, and I'm here to live with you." Your answer would be an emphatic, "NO!"

Now would I be justified in calling you mean-spirited? Would I be justified in saying that you were un-loving by not bringing this man whom you know nothing about into your home?

But, consider this, suppose your grown son or daughter comes to you and says, "Mom, Dad, I'm going through a hard time right now. Can I stay with you?" Every loving parent would instantly say, "By all means, come inside."

Why would you do that? Because you have a **relationship** with them! They are your sons and daughters. They belong to you.

Many people think that they can somehow just show up at Heaven's gate and say, "Ok God, I'm here! Let me in! I've tried to live a good life!" They think that just because they've been a good person they can just simply stroll right into Heaven. But we wouldn't expect to gain entrance anywhere else with that same kind of thought!

Imagine saying to some border patrol officer of some other country, "Hey, let me in! I'm a good person! I deserve to enter into your country."

They would say, "Buster, I don't care if you were a Boy Scout, let me see your passport."

In the same way, the only people who will get into Heaven are those who have their names written in the Lamb's book of Life. (Revelation 13:8) Can you imagine people who, in this life, have no time for God, no desire for God, no hunger for God, they can't stand the thought of going to church and learning about God—dying and ending up in an eternal church service where 12:00 never comes. Where they are surrounded by millions of people who are praising and worshipping a God whom they never knew or never cared for. They would be like a fish out of water! They don't belong.

It is doubtful whether people who don't love God could actually enjoy Heaven. Dallas Willard quips, "The question is not whether you will go to Heaven when you die. The question is whether you would like it if they let you in. God will be there, and you won't be able to get away from Him."

Love demands a choice

In a real sense, God's love demands that we make a choice. Love is not true love if you don't have the option to refuse.

Imagine a man asking a woman if she would marry him and she repeatedly says "No." Suppose that he says, "Now look…I love you so much that I am going to force you to marry me. And I'm going to force you to spend the rest of your life with me," and he locks her into the basement of his home.

God does not send anyone to Hell—He simply gives them what they choose.

Now, would that be true love? Absolutely not! And God's love is never going to force anyone to choose Him. His love is never going to force anyone to go to Heaven who doesn't want to go.

God does not send anyone to Hell—He simply gives them what they **choose**. Anyone who wants to be near God can be. Anyone who wants to be far from God will be.

24

Hell is not so much a sentence of judgment that God passes on people who reject Him as much as it is the end of a path that is freely chosen in this life. Hell is simply a person getting what he has said all of his life, "No, God!" Because in Hell, that is exactly what that person gets—*no God*. It is simply the eternal fruit of an earthly life lived apart from God.

C.S. Lewis said, "There are only two kinds of people in the end: those who say to God, "Thy will be done," and those to whom God says, in the end, "Thy will be done." All that are in Hell, choose it. Without that self-choice there could be no Hell. No soul that seriously and constantly desires joy will ever miss it. Those who seek find. To those who knock it is opened.'"[3]

Ted Turner once said, "I don't want anybody to die for me. I've had a few drinks and a few girlfriends and if that's going to put me in hell, well, then so be it."

The world thinks that if a person goes to Hell it's because they robbed, they murdered, or they raped—but Jesus died for all of those sins. The only sin that will send anyone to Hell is the unpardonable sin, which is refusing to accept God's free gift of eternal life through Jesus Christ our Lord.

We will fear death if we face it unknown, if we face it unatoned, but also…

We Will Fear Death
If We Face It Alone

What do people think about, just before they die? Here is one man's story:

Old Fred's hospital bed is surrounded by well-wishers, but it doesn't look good. Suddenly, he motions frantically to the pastor for something to write on. The pastor lovingly hands him a pen and a piece of paper. Fred uses his last bit of energy to scribble a note, and then he dies.

The pastor thinks it best not to look at the note right away, so he places it in his jacket pocket. At Fred's funeral, as the pastor is finishing his eulogy, he realizes he's wearing the jacket he was wearing when Fred died.

"Fred handed me a note just before he died," he says. "I haven't looked at it, but knowing Fred, I'm sure there's a word of inspiration in it for us all."

Opening the note, he reads aloud, "Help! You're standing on my oxygen hose!"[4]

When you come to the moment of your death…

- It's not going to matter if you have a million dollars in the bank.

- You are not going to care if you have lots of property and stocks.

- All that really matters when you come to death is this: Do you know Jesus?

It doesn't matter how much you know about Heaven. If there is not an ongoing relationship with Jesus Christ where you are walking in an intimate relationship with Him, then it would be expected that you would fear death.

The Psalmist said, "*Even though I walk through the valley of the shadow of death, I'll fear no evil…*" *Why did David not fear death? Because he was acutely aware of this fact:* "*… for Thou art with me*!" (Psalm 23:4)

When you know for certain that you are one of God's children and you walk with Him every day; you talk with Him every day; you study His Word every day; you take sin seriously and walk with integrity every day — then you don't fear death because, like David, you

C. S. Lewis said, "There are only two kinds of people in the end: those who say to God, "Thy will be done," and those to whom God says, in the end, "Thy will be done."

27

are aware of His presence being with you. Paul said, *"For I am convinced that neither death nor life…will be able to separate us from the love of God that is in Christ Jesus our Lord."* (Romans 8:38-39).

If you want to have God in your death, invite Him into your life.

If you want to know God when you die, meet Him while you are alive. There is no hint in Scripture of anyone who will have a second opportunity to be saved after death. And, no one who calls upon the name of the Lord in this life will be turned away. (Romans 10:13)

Is a "deathbed salvation" possible?

The short answer to this question is "yes." The most vivid example of this would be the thief on the cross who was dying next to Jesus (see Luke 23:43). As one of the thieves was dying on the cross next to Christ, there was something that he saw that sparked his faith. He said, "Lord, remember me when you go into your kingdom." And Jesus answered him, "Today, you will be with me in Paradise." Just moments before he would enter into eternity, his faith in Jesus saved him.

We, too, must make the same decision those two thieves who were dying next to Jesus had to make. Are we going to *receive* God's gift of salvation or are we going to *reject* Him. To not make a decision is to have made a decision. Which side of the cross are you on?

It is no more or less trouble for God to save a nine year old boy or a ninety year old woman.

So, yes, deathbed conversions are possible. However, I'm convinced that deathbed salvations are very rare.

Normally, people die just like they live. As a pastor, I have been with many people as they died. I have talked to many others who have talked to dying people about God. They know they are close to the door of death. They know they are going to die. They know they are lost in sin—and yet there is a hardness that comes over their hearts.

This is why the Bible says, *"Seek the LORD while he may be found; call on him while he is near."* Isaiah 55:6 (NIV) And, *"Now is the day of salvation."* 1 Corinthians 6:2. I looked up that word **now** in the Greek. It means **right now**.

I'm convinced that deathbed salvations are very rare.

If you have not yet made this decision, you are living on borrowed time right now. To ignore God's pull on your heart when you sense that He may be drawing you to believe in Him and to receive His offer of salvation is a very dangerous thing. The Bible indicates that your heart can grow hardened to the conviction and voice of the Holy Spirit if you procrastinate. There is a danger that you may die before you come to this opportunity again. That is why the Bible says, "*Behold, now is the accepted time. Today is the day of salvation.*"

Many people justify their excuse by saying, "Well, I'm just not ready to make that decision. Not today." But what they are really saying is, "Jesus, no thank you."

When a person says, "Not now" to Jesus – he is really saying, "Jesus, as far as right now is concerned, you are a liar. As far as right now is concerned I don't want to have anything to do with your plan of salvation."

It is a slap in the face of a holy God to say, "Lord, you just wait on me. I'll come around someday…maybe."

Your eternity is worth thinking long and hard about. The universal problem that we all have is death. Only a fool would go through life unprepared for something he knows is inevitable.

For those who know Jesus personally, God has promised to walk with us through that valley of the shadow of death. We all have wondered, "What will it be like for a Christian to die?" I think the best answer to that question does not come from a theologian but from a mother whose ten-year-old son was dying of cancer. He had leukemia and although the doctors did everything they could within their power to save him—his body was losing the battle with each day that passed. Charlie knew he was dying and one night as he was being tucked into bed, he asked his mother the question that no parent is adequately prepared to answer when their own child is facing an inevitable death. Charlie asked, "Mommy, what will it be like when I finally die?"

This mother paused for a moment while she breathed a quick prayer to God for wisdom as to what to say and then suddenly she had this thought. She said, "Charlie, do you remember all those times when you would fall asleep in the car on the way home from a late night outing or on the couch when you were up late on a Friday night watching TV? When you woke up, you didn't find yourself still in the car or laying on the couch did you? You found yourself lying on your own bed. But do you know how you got there? Your father would come in and he would lovingly scoop you up into his arms, and carry you upstairs and carefully tuck you into your own bed so that when you woke up you would be in a safe and comfortable place."

Mother said, "Charlie, I think death is a lot like that. There is going to come a day when you will simply fall asleep, but you will not be alone. Your Mommy and Daddy will be right there beside you. But most importantly, your Heavenly Father will be there too. And He will come and scoop you up into His love and caring arms, and when you wake up you will be in a wonderful and safe place called Heaven. And don't worry about us, Charlie. We'll see you in the morning."

Listen very carefully. The death clock is ticking. Everyone who calls upon the name of the Lord will be saved. Everyone who wants their sins forgiven will be forgiven. Everyone who wants to spend eternity near God will spend eternity near God.

Where do you want to spend eternity?

CHAPTER 2
The Highlights of Heaven

*"To go to heaven, fully to enjoy God,
is infinitely better than the most pleasant
accommodations here."*
- Jonathan Edwards

The Bible commands us to, "*Set your hearts on things above, where Christ is, seated at the right hand of God*." Colossians 3:1 (NIV) The word translated *set* is a strong one and is most commonly translated *seek* as it is in these verses:

- *"But seek first the kingdom of God and his righteousness, and all these things will be added to you*." Matthew 6:33

- "*Ask, and it will be given to you; seek, and you will find; knock, and it will be opened to you*." Matthew 7:7

- *"For the Son of Man came to seek and to save the lost*." Luke 19:10

The word is used in Luke 15:8 to describe the woman who searched for the lost coin. The New Living puts it this way, "*Set your sights on the realities of Heaven*."

Why set your heart on Heaven? Some fear if we are too Heavenly minded we will be of no earthly good. Randy Alcorn quotes Lewis in addressing this concern.

"If you read history, you will find that the Christians who did the most for the present world were just those who thought the most of the next. The Apostles, themselves, who set ablaze the conversion of the Roman Empire, the great men who built up the Middle Ages, the English Evangelicals who abolished the Slave Trade, all left their mark on Earth, precisely because their minds were occupied with Heaven. It is since Christians have largely ceased to think of the other world that they have become so ineffective in this. Aim at Heaven and you will get earth 'thrown in': aim at earth and you will get neither."[5]

Every Christian ought to be *looking, longing, and living* for Heaven! Billy Sunday once said, "If we could get a real appreciation of what Heaven is like, we would all be so homesick for Heaven, the devil wouldn't have a friend left on earth." John MacArthur: "We don't seek to escape this life by dreaming of heaven. But we do find we can endure this life because of the certainty of heaven."[6]

It would be impossible for God to give us an exhaustive description of what Heaven is going to be like. The Bible says, "*No eye has seen, no ear has heard, nor has entered into the heart of man those things which God prepared for those who love him*" (1 Corinthians 2:9).

Fully understanding Heaven is beyond our imagination. But, it never hurts to try.

Why we need to study Heaven? What difference does it make? I can think of at least three reasons:

1. Heaven gives us hope.

Life is hard. Life will always be hard. Yet studying the topic of Heaven gives us hope. This world is not our home. He is preparing a place for us. Someday soon, He will wipe away every tear from our eyes.

Watch a movie like *Twelve Years a Slave* and you are reminded of the horrible conditions of slavery in the South during that time in America's history. How did Christian slaves survive such horrible conditions? They wrote and sang songs about Heaven:

> *I've got shoes, you've got a-shoes*
>
> *All of God's children got shoes*
>
> *When I get to Heaven goin' to put on my shoes*
>
> *Goin' to walk all over God's Heaven*
>
> *I've got a harp, you've got a harp*
>
> *All of God's children got a harp*
>
> *When I get to Heaven goin' to play on my harp*
>
> *Goin' to play all over God's Heaven*

Singing songs about Heaven helped them get through the horrible conditions of that day. It can help you as well. Billy Graham says, "No matter what we're facing, we know it is only temporary, and ahead of us is Heaven."[7]

The hope of Heaven gives us hope when life is hard. It also warns us not to get too attached to the good things in this world. Joni Eareckson Tada says, "Let's not get too settled in, too satisfied with the good things down here on earth. They are only the tinkling sounds of the orchestra warming up. The real song is about to break into a heavenly symphony, and its prelude is only a few moments away."[8]

2. The hope of Heaven helps us face death.

We are all going to die. Our loved ones are all going to die. When you face death, I hope you have a strong hope in Heaven. When you have a general idea of what is awaiting us in Heaven, it helps to not only absolve our fear of death but it also makes us eager to meet the life that is to come.

3. The hope of Heaven motivates us to tell people about Heaven.

Just as death is real, Heaven and Hell are real. Ignorance doesn't make it go away. Ignoring it won't make it go away. Anyone who wants to be close to God can be. Anyone who wants their sins forgiven can have their sins forgiven. "*But how can they call on him to save them unless they believe in him? And how can they believe in him if they have never heard about him? And how can they hear about him unless someone tells them?*" Romans 10:14 (NLT)

A boy looked up at a beautiful night sky and said to his dad, "If Heaven looks so beautiful on the outside, imagine how beautiful it is on the inside!"

I'd like to answer eight Frequently Asked Questions (FAQs) about Heaven.

What is the difference between the present Heaven and the future Heaven?

The Bible teaches that if we are in Christ, we go immediately to Heaven when we die. However, the Heaven we experience immediately is not the same Heaven we will experience forever.

What we usually think of when we hear the word "Heaven" is what theologians call the *intermediate* Heaven. When we die, we immediately go into the presence of God until our bodily resurrection. (See Isaiah 65:17; Isaiah 66:22; 2 Peter 3:13; Revelation 21:1). Our Christian loved ones who have died are in this present, intermediate Heaven.

This is not the same thing as purgatory. Purgatory does not exist; the Bible never speaks of it. The Catholic concept of Purgatory is a place where people, "undergo purification, so as to achieve the holiness necessary to enter the joy of Heaven."[9] The Bible says, "*If we confess our sins, he is faithful and just and will forgive us our sins and purify us from all unrighteousness.*" 1 John 1:9 (NIV) We don't go to Purgatory to be purified. We are purified right now by confessing our sins and receiving God's forgiveness.

When we die, we go to Heaven, but it is not the ultimate Heaven. Revelation says there will be a new Heaven and a new earth. We will enter into this new Heaven after our bodily resurrection. Randy Alcorn emphasizes this point:[10]

> *It bears repeating because it is so commonly misunderstood: When we die, believers in Christ will not go to the Heaven where we'll live forever. Instead, we'll go to an intermediate Heaven. In the intermediate Heaven, we'll await the time of Christ's return to the earth, our bodily resurrection, the final judgment, and the creation of the new Heavens and New Earth. If we fail to grasp this truth, we will fail to understand the biblical doctrine of Heaven.*

The word for *new* in Revelation 21 teaches that Heaven will not just be new as opposed to old. It will be different. It speaks of a change in quality.[11]

Our loved ones that have passed away will not experience this New Heaven and New Earth before us.

Revelation 21:16 describes this New Heaven as a cube. It is 1,400 miles on each side. I live in Kansas City. 1,400 miles is about the distance from Kansas City to the west coast. That is the dimension of one side of the new Heaven. You could fit a building 600,000 stories high inside.

What will Heaven be like?

We tend to think of Heaven as someone playing a harp on a puffy cloud somewhere. We say that people there are at rest. It doesn't sound like they are having a lot of fun. Someone told me once, "When I think of Heaven, I kind of get depressed."

A Greek Philosopher named Aristides, who was not a believer, described Christians at a funeral in 125 AD: "This religion is successful because if any righteous man among the Christians passes from this world, they rejoice and offer thanks to God and

The Bible teaches that if we are in Christ, we go immediately to Heaven when we die.

they escort his body with songs and thanksgiving as if he were setting out from this place to eternity."[12]

The early church saw death as a graduation—a time of celebration and joy. That is how death was perceived by the early church. It was visible, even to those who were not followers of Christ.

Some people feel more at home in the country whereas others gravitate more towards large cities. I find it interesting that the Bible is depicted as both a city and a country – it's the best of both worlds.

Heaven is described as a city. Hebrews 11:10 says, *"For he was looking forward to the city that has foundations, whose designer and builder is God."* This may be a little fanciful, but when I picture the city of Heaven, I picture that scene in Star Wars where flying cars are zipping down invisible lanes far above the streets. It will be a place of action, a place of lights, a place of activity, a place of excitement. Everything good about a city will be there, and none of the bad. No crime; no pollution, no traffic jams. But, the throbbing energy of the city will be there in full force.

Heaven is described as a country. If you don't like the hubbub of the city, I have good news. Heaven is described as the country. If you prefer fresh air to city lights, Heaven will be Heaven for you. *"But as it is, they desire a better country, that is, a Heavenly one."* Hebrews 11:16 There will be rivers and mountains and trees and flowers. If you enjoy hiking, this will be the place for you.

Heaven is described as a garden. Jesus told the thief on the cross, *"Today you will be with me in paradise."* (Luke 23:43) Randy Alcorn points out that *paradise* speaks of a garden:[13]

> *The word paradise comes from the Persian word pairidaeza, meaning "a walled park" or "enclosed garden." It was used to describe the great walled*

gardens of the Persian king Cyrus's royal palaces. In the Septuagint, the Greek translation of the Old Testament, the Greek word for paradise is used to describe the Garden of Eden (e.g., Genesis 2:8; Ezekiel 28:13). Later, because of the Jewish belief that God would restore Eden, paradise became the word to describe the eternal state of the righteous, and to a lesser extent, the intermediate Heaven.

The word paradise does not refer to wild nature but to nature under mankind's dominion. The garden or park was not left to grow entirely on its own. People brought their creativity to bear on managing, cultivating, and presenting the garden or park. "The idea of a walled garden," writes Oxford professor Alister McGrath, "enclosing a carefully cultivated area

If you prefer fresh air to city lights, Heaven will be Heaven for you.

of exquisite plants and animals, was
the most powerful symbol of paradise
available to the human imagination,
mingling the images of the beauty
of nature with the orderliness of
human construction. . . . The whole
of human history is thus enfolded in
the subtle interplay of sorrow over a
lost paradise, and the hope of its final
restoration."

Genesis starts with a garden and Revelation ends with a garden.

So, whether you like the hustle and bustle of the city, the peace and quiet of the country, or the beauty of a garden, there will be something for you in Heaven.

What will we look like in Heaven?

The best answer to this question is based on what we observe about Jesus and His resurrection body. Jesus's resurrected body was a real, physical body that allowed him to walk, talk, and eat. (John 21, Luke 24)

We are told that our bodies will be just like His. "***Just as we have borne the image of the man of dust, we shall also bear the image of the man of Heaven***." 1 Corinthians 15:49 John MacArthur says, "In heaven we will have real bodies—changed, glorified, made like Christ's resurrection body—real, eternal bodies, just as His was real." [14]

Jesus' resurrected body is a model for what our resurrected body will be like. This puts to rest the myth that we will be wispy ghosts playing harps on the clouds. We will have real, physical bodies and will be in a real, physical place.

Imagine having a brand new body with no pain, no weakness, no suffering, no disease, no osteoporosis, no diabetes, and no blemishes. Some have speculated that since Jesus was thirty three years old when He died and was resurrected, that our resurrected body will look similar to that age.

In the book *Heaven is for Real,* Todd Burpo describes the near death experience of his son Colton. One interesting detail of the story is that Colton describes seeing his grandfather, whom he has never met. He recognizes a picture of him that was taken fifty years earlier—when his grandfather was about thirty three.

There will be no time in Heaven, so a thirty three year old won't have the same meaning it has for us. Our bodies will be eternally in their prime.

Do you remember the show *Extreme Makeover*? They take the ugliest person you have ever seen and turn them into stunning beauties. The before-and-after was night and day. Compared to Heaven, the most beautiful person you have ever seen is the before picture. In Heaven, He will make all things new. We will all be beautiful, fit, and healthy.

Note something else we learn from Jesus' resurrection body. Just as the disciples had no trouble recognizing the resurrected Jesus, people will have no trouble recognizing you. I wonder if they will ask, "Have you lost weight?" For a lot of folks, that alone would make it heavenly.

Will there be children in Heaven?

You may have had a still born child or a miscarriage. Will you be able to see that baby in Heaven? Look at this passage from Isaiah:

The wolf shall dwell with the lamb,

and the leopard shall lie down with the young goat,

and the calf and the lion and the fattened calf together;

and a little child shall lead them.

The cow and the bear shall graze;

their young shall lie down together;

and the lion shall eat straw like the ox.

The nursing child shall play over the hole of the cobra,

and the weaned child shall put his hand on the adder's den.

They shall not hurt or destroy in all my holy mountain;

for the earth shall be full of the knowledge of the LORD as the waters cover the sea.

Isaiah 11:6–9

Some theologians believe that children who die will enter Heaven as children. From there, they will grow into maturity. If this is so, believing parents will have the opportunity to see the childhood they missed on earth. Many opportunities that are lost in this life will be recaptured in the next.

One of the many compelling parts of the book *Heaven Is for Real* is the section where little Colton tells of meeting his unborn sister. Todd's wife had a miscarriage before Colton was born. When Colton went to Heaven, he met her. He describes her as a child, "'She looked a lot like Cassie,' [his sister] Colton said. 'She is just a little bit smaller, and she has dark hair.'"[15]

What are we going to do in Heaven?

The greatest pleasure in Heaven will be fellowship with God, just as it was with Adam and Eve in the Garden of Eden.

At the same time, Heaven will be a busy place. It is not only a place of resting, it is a place of ruling. Heaven is not only a place of leisure, it is also a place of labor. Revelation 22:3 says, "*His servants shall serve Him*." (NIV)

In the parable of the minas, Jesus says to the man who doubled his five minas, "*And he said to him, 'And you are to be over five cities*.'" Luke 19:19 The context has to do with the Eternal Kingdom and suggests that we will have a great work to do in Heaven. 2 Timothy 2.12 says, "*We will also reign with Him*."

I think the average Christian sees Heaven is an eternal retirement home. That is not biblical. Heaven will be a very active place. There will be places to go and people to see and things to do. I say this reverently: Heaven will be fun. I wouldn't be surprised to see motorcycles and snow skiing and tennis. There won't be golf. It couldn't be heaven if there were golf. Too frustrating!

Our God is a God of productivity and Heaven will be a place of doing. Our God is a creative God and Heaven will be a creative place. We will build things, draw things, and make art and music. **Joni Eareckson Tada** says, "All the earthly things we enjoy with our friends here will find their more exalted expression in heaven."[16]

We will have renewed minds, as well as renewed bodies. We will be people full of energy and clearheaded thinking. Our vision and hearing will be perfect. We will be eager to take on new projects and will have the energy to complete them. Whatever a great day at work feels like for you, Heaven will be a little bit like that. We will exercise leadership and authority in making important decisions. We will have ideas and the energy to carry out those ideas.

Heaven will be a place of rest. God gives a pattern for rest. He created the world in six days, and on the seventh day, He rested. Heaven will include both work and rest.

The rest of Heaven will be different than the rest here. It will be totally relaxing. We will be able to sit down by a river and not think about work. In Heaven, rest will be worry-free.

Will we know everything when we get to Heaven?

No. Only God is omniscient. However, we will see things with clarity. Paul said, "*For now we see in a mirror dimly, but then face to face. Now I know in part; then I shall know fully, even as I have been fully known.*" 1 Corinthians 13:12 We won't have any misconceptions in Heaven. Our thinking will be error-free, but we won't know everything.

The greatest pleasure in Heaven will be fellowship with God.

Heaven will be a place where we are consistently learning and growing in our knowledge about everything God has created in our universe. This is exciting to me because I love to learn. The joy of learning will be part of the joy of Heaven. In Heaven we will have all of eternity to learn. If you've ever wanted to get a Master's degree, you will have time to do so in Heaven. If you want to learn to play guitar, there will be plenty of time for that Heaven. Would you like to learn a foreign language? There will be time for that as well.

The Bible teaches that Angels don't know everything, and long to learn. (1 Peter 1:12) Angels have been around for eternity, and they still don't know everything. They are still learning.

Jesus will be our primary teacher in Heaven. "… *and raised us up with him and seated us with Him in the Heavenly places in Christ Jesus, so that in the coming ages He might show the immeasurable riches of His grace in kindness toward us in Christ Jesus.*" Ephesians 2:6–7 Do you enjoy a good Bible study? Imagine being taught by Jesus!

One of my favorite stories is the post-resurrection story of the disciples talking to Jesus on the Emmaus road. Jesus did a little Bible study with them, "*And beginning with Moses and all the Prophets, he interpreted to them in all the Scriptures the things concerning himself.*" Luke 24:27 I have often thought how wonderful it would have been to be with Jesus that day. In Heaven, we will have all eternity to walk with Jesus and have Him explain the Scriptures.

Heaven will be a place that is anything but boring. It will be a place of discovery. It will be eternally interesting, just as God is infinitely fascinating. Joni Eareckson Tada says, "For when it comes to heaven, there is no limit to what the Lord will confide to those whose faith is rooted in Scripture."[17]

What won't be in Heaven?

Randy Alcorn has written what is, perhaps, the best book ever written on Heaven. The full volume is 560 pages. He did a follow-up called *Heaven: Biblical Answers to Common Questions,* which is only sixty pages. In it, he speaks eloquently about what will not be in Heaven:[18]

No death, no suffering. No funeral homes, abortion clinics, or psychiatric wards. No rape, missing children, or drug rehabilitation centers. No bigotry, no muggings or killings. No worry or depression or economic downturns. No wars, no unemployment. No anguish over failure and miscommunication. No con men. No locks. No death. No mourning. No pain. No boredom.

No arthritis, no handicaps, no cancer, no taxes, no bills, no computer crashes, no weeds, no bombs, no drunkenness, no traffic jams and accidents, no septic-tank backups. No mental illness. No unwanted e-mails.

Close friendships but no cliques, laughter but no put-downs. Intimacy, but no temptation to immorality. No hidden agendas, no backroom deals, no betrayals.

Imagine mealtimes full of stories, laughter, and joy, without fear of insensitivity, inappropriate behavior, anger, gossip, lust, jealousy, hurt feelings, or anything that eclipses joy. That will be Heaven.

There won't be churches or temples in the new universe, not because they're bad, but because they won't be necessary. We won't need to be drawn into God's presence. We'll live there, constantly and consciously. We'll thank God profoundly, and worship and praise him together, whether we're working in a garden, singing, riding bikes, or drinking coffee (no reason to think there won't be coffee trees on the New Earth).

Revelation 21:4 is a classic: "**He will wipe away every tear from their eyes, and death shall be no more, neither shall there be mourning, nor crying, nor pain anymore, for the former things have passed away.**"

As I was preparing this material, my son was fishing in the backyard. We have a lake on our property and he enjoys fishing. He cast his line into the water, and the fishing pole slipped out of his hand. We attempted to retrieve it, but to no avail.

I sat down to try to comfort my son in his tears, and in the back of my mind I was thinking about this passage. No more tears. In this life there are plenty of tears for him to look forward to. In this world we will have trouble. There will be pain; there will be sorrow. But Jesus has gone to prepare a place for us where there will be none of that.

Jesus said, "*Blessed are those who mourn, for they shall be comforted.*" Matthew 5:4

Will we recognize loved ones in Heaven?

Yes! We will know more in Heaven than we know now, not less. Of course we will recognize one another. We will even remember all of their names!

Being with Christ will be the greatest joy in Heaven. The second greatest joy will be reuniting with loved ones. We will know them. We will remember things that happened here on earth.

At the transfiguration, Peter, James, and John recognized Moses and Elijah, even though they had never seen them. They weren't introduced to them as strangers; they recognized them.

This suggests we will instantly recognize people we know about but have not met. If we will recognize them, surely we will recognize people we know.

Eternity is forever. We will have all eternity to meet and get to know everyone in Heaven. We can hear their stories and they can hear ours. I have a long list of people I want to meet. I have a long list of people who have passed away and I want to see them again. I bet you do too.

Although we will recognize people in Heaven, we will not be married in Heaven. Jesus makes that very clear. "***For in the resurrection they neither marry nor are given in marriage, but are like angels in Heaven.***" Matthew 22:30 The only marriage in Heaven is between the Bridegroom, Jesus Christ, and His Bride the church.

Think how weird it would be if there were marriage in Heaven. Suppose you had been married more than once, who would you be married to in Heaven? There will be no marriage in Heaven.

The story is told of an old man who had a rough relationship with his ex-wife. When he got to Heaven he met St. Peter who informed him he had to pass a one-word spelling test to get into Heaven. "What is the word?"

"Love. Spell love and you can get into Heaven."

"L-O-V-E."

"You passed. You are in."

Then, St. Peter surprised him by asking him to man the desk as he needed to step away for a bit. The man agreed. Peter explained that he just needed to give anyone who showed up a one-word spelling test as he had received.

Just then, the ex-wife showed up. "You will need to take a one-word spelling test before you can get in."

"O.K. What is the word?"

"Czechoslovakia."

Well, here is some good news: all our conflict will be behind us in Heaven. Strained relationships will be behind us.

In Heaven you will know and be known. The Bible says, "*For now we see in a mirror dimly, but then face to face. Now I know in part; then I shall know fully, even as I have been fully known*." 1 Corinthians 13:12

Being with Christ will be the greatest joy in Heaven. The second greatest joy will be reuniting with loved ones.

What is the best thing about Heaven?

The best thing about Heaven is that Jesus will be there. Revelation 22:4 says that we will see His face. As the old hymn writer put it, "Oh that will be glory for me!"

The light of Heaven is the face of Jesus.
The music of Heaven is the theme of Jesus.
The employment of Heaven is the service of Jesus.
The joy of Heaven is the presence of Jesus.
The fullness of Heaven is the person of Jesus.

This story is told of a young boy who was born blind. He had never seen a sunset or a rose or his mother's face. A surgery was developed that was able to cure his blindness. When they took off the bandages he could not believe what he was seeing. Everything was so beautiful. Imagine what it would be like to see the blue sky for the first time, and to see the green grass for the first time. Beaming, he exclaimed, "Mother, why didn't you tell me it would be so beautiful!"

His mother replied, "I tried to, Son. I guess you just had to see it for yourself."

In this chapter I have tried to explain as best I could the beauty of Heaven. But this explanation pales in comparison to the real thing. You will just have to see it for yourself!

CHAPTER 3
The Horrors of Hell

"Not believing in Hell doesn't lower the temperature down there one degree."
- Neil T. Anderson

A lot of people today are putting a question mark after Hell. They are questioning whether a loving God could send people to an eternity in Hell. Or, they believe in Hell, but they see it as an embarrassing side of God. A recent book was released whose title has this sentiment: *Hell is Real (But I Hate to Admit it).*

Perhaps you think it doesn't matter. It does. *The Evangelical Dictionary of Theology* says, "Jesus spoke of Hell more often than did anyone else in the New Testament. And nowhere is there a hint of any possible reversal of the last judgment."[19] Jesus spoke often of Hell, so it must be important. Jesus spoke more on the subject of Hell than he spoke on the subject of Heaven. The reason there is so much Hell in our world is there is so little Hell in our pulpits.

Hell is real. We need to sound the alarm. We need to ring the bell. We need to tell people. We need to speak up before it is too late.

Paul said, *"Knowing, therefore, the terror of the Lord, we persuade men."* 2 Corinthians 5:11a (NKJV) R.T. Kendall said, "The teachings of Jesus on Hell were not meant to make us comfortable."[20]

William Booth, founder of the Salvation Army had an evangelism program that was the envy of the church in his day. He was asked how it could be better. "If all my soldiers could spend just five minutes in Hell, that would be the best training for our soldiers."[21]

The Reality of Hell

The reality of Hell is being frozen out by preachers who do not mention it in their pulpits. A report in the Los Angeles Times revealed that talking about Hell from today's pulpits is, "at an all-time low."[22] You can go to a lot of churches and attend for years without hearing Hell mentioned. Why is this? Perhaps it is our theology of Hell.

I'd like to mention four views of Hell before we look at what the Bible says.

Some say Hell is what we create on this earth. A young woman came crying to her mother. Her mother asked why she was crying. "I can't marry George. He doesn't believe in Hell."

Her mother replied, "Go ahead and marry him. He will come to believe in Hell after he is married to you!"

Hell is more than a bad marriage. It is more than a bad day. It is worse than a bad life. It is a real, physical place of unending, conscious torment.

In *The Forbidden Woman,* Malika Mokeddem, said, "Hell is every day. It's now."[23] She is wrong. It is far worse than anything in this life.

A second view of Hell is annihilationism. This view holds that when you die, you die. You are like a dog. When you die, you simply cease to exist. There is no punishment or consequences for sin.

The Bible teaches no such thing. In Revelation 20:14 it describes Hell as a lake of fire—a place of eternal punishment for those who reject Christ.

A third view is universalism. The logic goes like this: because God is good, and because God is loving, He will eventually welcome all people into Heaven. The Bible does not teach this. "*And the smoke of their torment goes up forever and ever, and they have no rest, day or night, these worshipers of the beast and its image, and whoever receives the mark of its name.*" Revelation 14:11

There is a fourth view you may not be familiar with. It is called the conditionalist view. This is taught by Edward Fudge and holds that the fires of Hell are eternal, but the people who are thrown there are punished for a time, but then burn up. The name conditionalist comes from the belief that eternal life is conditional upon faith. Man in his natural state is not eternal. He is given eternal life when he is saved. When the Bible says that the gift of God is eternal life, Conditionalists take this to mean that if you don't receive the gift of eternal life, you don't live eternally.

This may sound like annihilationism, but it has this key difference. Conditionalists believe that unbelievers will be punished for a time, in keeping with their sinfulness.

Then, eventually, they will perish. They take the word **perish** of John 3:16 quite literally. When Romans 6:23 says that the wages of sin is death, they take death in the literal sense, rather than spiritual death of separation from God. This view stands mid-way between the Annihilationists view and the traditional view.

Jesus on Hell

Jesus taught that Hell is a literal place. Jesus called it eternal fire and eternal punishment. Jesus spoke fifty-three times on the topic of Hell. He spoke of Hell in His first sermon, and He spoke of Hell in His last sermon. Jesus taught that you can be assured that there is a Heaven and He has gone there to prepare it for us. He also taught that there is a Hell and you do not want to go there.

If we cannot count on the truthfulness of Jesus' words on Hell, then we cannot count on anything else Jesus said.

Sometimes we make fun of "Hellfire, and brimstone" preachers. Be careful. Jesus was one of those preachers. And, we don't ridicule a doctor that warns of cancer. Hell is a reality. Love demands that we talk about it.

Dr. Maurice Rawlings was a cardiologist and a professor of medicine at the University of Tennessee. He was a devout atheist. He considered all religion to be hocus-pocus. For him, death was nothing more than a painless extinction. Theologically, we would say he was an annihilationist.

All that changed in 1977 when Dr. Rawlings was resuscitating a man who had come back from the edge of death. The man was absolutely terrified. Dr. Rawlings wrote in his journal, "Each time he regained heartbeat and respiration, the patient screamed, "I am in Hell!" He was terrified and pleaded with me to help him. I was scared to death.… Then I noticed a genuinely alarmed look on his face. He had a terrified look worse than the expression seen in death! This patient had a grotesque grimace expressing sheer horror! His pupils were dilated, and he was perspiring and trembling—he looked as if his hair was on end."[24]

Each time he was revived, he was anguished: "Don't stop! Don't you understand? I'm in Hell! Each time you quit I go back to Hell … How do I stay out of Hell?"

An unbeliever at the time, Rawlings replied, "I'm busy. Don't bother me about your Hell until I finish getting this pacemaker into place." But he soon saw that his patient was immersed in extreme panic. Despite his own doubts about God and the reality of an afterlife, Rawlings told the man he should ask for God's forgiveness and turn over his life to God. They prayed together—the dying man and the agnostic—on the clinic floor. Soon, the man's condition stabilized, and he was transported to the hospital.[25]

Rawlings himself eventually became a committed Christian as a result of the experience.

Rawlings later did some research on Near Death Experiences. It has been popularly reported that nearly all Near Death Experiences were positive—visions of light and such. He interviewed the man in the story about a week later and was shocked to discover the man had no recollection with his brush with death. Rawlings concluded that the brush with Hell was so horrific the mind blocked out the memory.

Further researched revealed that when they examined more closely, about fifty percent of Near Death Experiences are, in fact, negative. People see lakes of fire and devil-like figures. Dr. Rawlings said, "Just listening to these patients has changed my whole life. There is a life after death, and if I don't know where I'm going, it's not safe to die."[26]

If you do not believe in the existence of Hell, you will five seconds after you die.

The Residents of Hell

"*Then he will say to those on his left, 'Depart from me, you cursed, into the eternal fire prepared for the devil and his angels.*'" Matthew 25:41

Man was not made for Hell, and Hell was not made for man. Hell was not created for human beings, it was created for Lucifer and his angels.

In Isaiah 14 we read that Satan tried to take over the throne of God, but was unsuccessful. So, God prepared Hell as a reminder of the consequences of rebellion.

Satan is not in Hell yet. The Bible says that Satan is the prince of the power of the air. It says he is at work in those who are disobedient (Ephesians 2:2). 2 Corinthians 4:4 refers to Satan as the God of this age. Satan and his demons are alive and well and active on planet earth. Invisible warfare is taking place all around us.

Satan is not in Hell, but he will be thrown there to be punished through all eternity. "*And the devil who had deceived them was thrown into the lake of fire and sulfur where the beast and the false prophet were, and they will be tormented day and night forever and ever.*" Revelation 20:10

Satan chose to set himself in opposition to God. Everyone, who will eventually go to Hell, will do so because they,

If you do not believe in the existence of Hell, you will five seconds after you die.

like Satan, set themselves in opposition to God. There will be no resident in Hell who has not rebelled against God. There will be no resident in Hell that loves God and wants to be near God. It will be true then as it is true now: you are as close to God as you want to be.

C.S. Lewis told about a tombstone that read, "Here lies an atheist—all dressed up and no place to go." Lewis quietly replied, "I bet he wishes that were so."[27]

Jesus made it very easy to avoid Hell. I can summarize it into two words: receive and believe. "*But to all who did receive Him, who believed in His name, He gave the right to become children of God.*" John 1:12 All you have to do to go to Heaven and not Hell is receive Jesus and believe on His name. Receive and believe. If someone asks you how they can miss Hell and get to Heaven, tell them it is simple: receive and believe. It is not enough to believe that God exists, the devils do that. (James 2:19) We must receive Him as our Savior and Lord.

A Hospice nurse was caring for the famous atheist, Voltaire, when he died. After he died she vowed never to care for an atheist as he died again. She said that as he was dying he screamed, "I am in Hell! I am in Hell! Please help me!" He pleaded for mercy from the same God he had spent his whole life fighting.

What did Jesus mean when He said, "*And if your right hand causes you to sin, cut it off and throw it away. For it is better that you lose one of your members than that your whole body go into Hell.*" Matthew 5:30

Jesus was not saying you have to cut off your hand to go to Heaven. He was saying that whatever price you have to pay, whatever it takes, whoever you have to offend, you do not want to go to Hell. Jesus was saying it would be better to be a maimed saint on your way to Heaven than a healthy sinner heading for Hell.

John described the residents of Hell this way: "*But as for the cowardly, the faithless, the detestable, as for murderers, the sexually immoral, sorcerers, idolaters, and all liars, their portion will be in the lake that burns with fire and sulfur, which is the second death.*" Revelation 21:8

Note the word cowardly in this verse. The cowardly are afraid to face the ridicule of following Christ. They are too afraid to stand up, stand up for Jesus. They are not willing to say, "Though none go with me, still I will follow."

I heard the gospel as a twelve year old boy listening to Bailey Smith preaching about the wheat and the tares. I came face to face with the reality that I was a sinner heading to a sinner's Hell. Everyone I knew thought I was a Christian, but I knew better. I had already been baptized. I was the "Bible-answer-man" in Sunday School. I knew all the answers. I was a good person. But I was not saved. I did not have a personal relationship with Jesus Christ. I was headed for Hell.

As Bailey Smith was preaching, I couldn't wait for him to shut up. I wanted him to be done, so that I could run down the aisle and publicly confess my faith in Jesus Christ. The strongest man alive could not have kept me from walking down the aisle. (By the way, you don't have to walk down an aisle to receive Christ. You can cry out to Him right now in prayer. For more details, see the last chapter of this book.)

I wanted to give my life to Christ because I knew what was at stake. My eternal destiny was hinged on this decision – to receive or to reject. I finally realized what

Jesus had done for me-- it was crystal clear. I wanted to receive the gift of eternal life.

And what was the result? Jesus changed me. He gave me the assurance of my salvation. I am 100% sure—I'm not going to Hell, I'm going to Heaven. He changed my heart. He cleansed me. He forgave all my sins. He wrote my name in the Lamb's Book of Life. He made a reservation for me in Heaven. And, now I have devoted the rest of my life to telling people how they can go to Heaven when they die.

The Bible says we can know for sure we are going to go to Heaven when we die. "*I write these things to you who believe in the name of the Son of God that you may know that you have eternal life.*" 1 John 5:13 In a moment, during a Bailey Smith revival, I came to know that I have eternal life. How wonderful life has been living with this confidence!

Don't be counted among the cowardly. Accept Christ. Stand up for Christ, no matter what it costs.

The Realm of Hell

The Bible uses four different words to describe Hell.

Sheol. This is the Hebrew word for Hell. "In ordinary usage it means ravine, chasm, underworld, or world of the dead. In the Old Testament it is the place where the dead have their abode, a hollow space underneath the earth where the dead are gathered in."[28]

Hades. This is the Greek word for Hell. This is the word that Jesus used in this passage, "*and in Hades, being in torment, he lifted up his eyes and saw Abraham far off and Lazarus at his side.*" Luke 16:23 It is a place of conscious torment and suffering. But, like the temporary Heaven, it is not the final resting place. It is a hellish holding cell until the final judgment at the Great White Throne. In Revelation 20:14 it says that, "*Death and Hades were thrown into the lake of fire. This is the second death, the lake of fire.*"

The Lake of Fire. People ask if this is a literal fire, or, if it is metaphorical? We have no indication to think of this as being a symbol or a metaphor. Quite frankly, if it is metaphorical, it is pointing to a reality that is so horrible the best way we can think of it is to think of being burned all over. R.C. Sproul said:[29]

> I suspect they are symbols, but I find no relief in that. We must not think of them as being merely symbols. It is probable that the sinner in Hell would prefer a literal

The Bible says we can know for sure we are going to go to Heaven when we die.

*lake of fire as his eternal abode to
the reality of Hell represented in the
lake of fire image. If these images
are indeed symbols, then we must
conclude that the reality is worse than
the symbol suggests. The function of
symbols is to point beyond themselves
to a higher or more intense state of
actuality than the symbol itself can
contain. That Jesus used the most
awful symbols imaginable to describe
Hell is no comfort to those who see
them simply as symbols.*

Gehenna. This is the Greek word Jesus used most often for Hell. Literally, the word referred to ***the valley of Hennom.*** It is a valley on the south side of Jerusalem where, in Old Testament days, human sacrifices were offered to the pagan god Molech. By Jesus' day, it was the city dump where fires were kept burning continuously. The dead bodies of animals and executed criminals were brought here to be burned. Maggots could be seen in Gehenna.

The stench of Gehenna was that of rotting, burning, flesh. At night you could sometimes hear dogs gnashing away at corpses on the edge of the fire. It was the most repugnant place in the known world at that time. This was the earthly metaphor Jesus used to describe a spiritual reality. The word is used twelve times in the New Testament, eleven of them from the lips of Jesus.

Let's look at the most descriptive picture we have of Hell:

> *The poor man died and was carried by the angels to Abraham's side. The rich man also died and was buried, and in Hades, being in torment, he lifted up his eyes and saw Abraham far off and Lazarus at his side. And he called out, 'Father Abraham, have mercy on me, and send Lazarus to dip the end of his finger in water and cool my tongue, for I am in anguish in this flame.' But Abraham said, 'Child, remember that you in your lifetime received your good things, and Lazarus in like manner bad things; but now he is comforted here, and you are in anguish. And besides all this, between us and you a great chasm has been fixed, in order that those who would pass from here to you may not be able, and none may cross from there to us.' And he said, 'Then I beg you, father, to send him to my father's house— for I have five brothers—so that he may warn them, lest they also come into this place of torment.' But Abraham said, 'They have Moses and the Prophets; let them hear them.' And he said, 'No, father Abraham, but if*

someone goes to them from the dead,
they will repent.' He said to him, 'If they
do not hear Moses and the Prophets,
neither will they be convinced if
someone should rise from the dead.'"
Luke 16:22–31

Allow me to draw your attention to several key words from this passage and others.

Torment. (Verse 23) Hell involves horrible physical pain. The word used for "torment" literally refers to a black stone used to torture people with the goal of extracting information. Think Jack Bauer on a rampage in the popular TV series, 24. Now think about enduring this type of torment…forever.

Agony. Thayer's Greek-English Lexicon of the New Testament describes this as, "to cause intense pain; to be in anguish, be tormented."[30]

As believers we will receive a new, resurrected body. Unbelievers will also receive a new body that will allow them to endure eternal punishment in Hell. Make no mistake. This rich man is in intense, unrelieved, tortuous, pain.

Memory. There is no Alzheimer's in Hell. Verse 25 says, "*Remember*…" This teaches us that those in Hell will be able to remember everything. Much of the agony of Hell will be knowing that things could have been different.

Luke 13.28 speaks of Hell as a place where there is weeping and gnashing of teeth. Gnashing of teeth has to do with regret. It has to do with, "if only." It has to do with memory.

One of the most haunting things about Hell is that a million years from now people will still remember and regret. They will think, "It didn't have to be this way. It could have been different. It could have been *so* different. If only..." Every regret in this life will be eternally remembered.

Maggots. Jesus described Hell this way: "*where their worm does not die and the fire is not quenched*." Mark 9:48 In the context, Jesus is speaking of Gehenna. It was literally a place that constantly bred worms. They were constantly gnawing on an unending supply of carcasses that were added to the heap. In Hell, the worms never die. The gnawing never stops.

Punishment. The Bible indicates that just as there will be degrees of reward in Heaven, so there will also be degrees of punishment in Hell. In my research, I found eighteen passages that indicate that there are different levels of punishment in Hell. Scripture says, "*But the one who did not know, and did what deserved a beating, will receive a light beating. Everyone to whom much was given, of him much will be required, and from him to whom they entrusted much, they will demand the more*." Luke 12:48

Fear. The Psalmist Asaph wrote says:

> *Surely You set them in slippery places;*
> *You cast them down to destruction.*
> *Oh, how they are brought to desolation,*
> *as in a moment!*
> *They are utterly consumed with terrors.*
> Psalm 73:18–19 (NKJV)

Have you ever been awakened at night due to a strange sound you heard in your house? You start to break out into a cold sweat and you strain to hear if the sound repeats itself again, but the only thing you can hear is the heartbeat that is pounding in your chest. The Bible says that Hell will be like that—eternally. *"They are utterly consumed with terrors."*

> *We can endure almost anything if we know there is a purpose.*

Sorrow. We looked at Luke 13:28 earlier where it refers to *"gnashing of teeth."* In that same verse it speaks of weeping. The word means, "to weep or wail, with emphasis upon the noise accompanying the weeping."[31] In Heaven, God will wipe away every tear; in Hell there will be endless crying, wailing, weeping.

Purposelessness. I am told that in prison camps, one of the punishments they sometimes give to prisoners has to do with this idea of purposelessness. The guards will make the prisoners dig a hole. For days they will be in the hot sun digging. When they are finished, the guards command them to fill the hole back up. Over and over they dig holes and fill them back. They have found that this purposeless work will break men down more than anything else.

We can endure almost anything if we know there is a purpose. We can put up with anything if there is a strong enough "why." In Hell there is no "why." There is no purpose.

One of the things that makes Heaven heavenly is that there will be purpose. We will have a job to do. We will have responsibilities. In Hell it is not so. There is no purpose. You may be somebody in this life. In Hell, you will be nobody. Ecclesiastes 9:10 says, "*No work or thought or knowledge or wisdom in Sheol, to which you are going.*"

Darkness. Matthew 25:30 describes Hell as a place of darkness. Jude spoke of, "*the gloom of utter darkness has been reserved forever.*" Jude 13 Those who die without Christ will never again see a glimmer of light.

In our world, there is rarely a time when we are in utter darkness. When you turn out the lights at night, you can often see some light coming in from streetlights or the moon outside. Many of our electronic devices have small lights that never go off. We don't think too much about it unless you go to a place of absolute darkness. Perhaps you have been spelunking in a cave and turned out all the lights. That is complete darkness. Hell will be like that forever.

A bottomless pit. Seven times in the book of Revelation, Hell is referred to as a bottomless pit. Here is one, "***The angel threw him into the bottomless pit, which He then shut and locked so Satan could not deceive the nations anymore until the thousand years were finished.***" Revelation 20:3 (NLT)

Bill Hybels describes it this way:[32]

> *The bottomless pit…conjures up dreamlike feelings of falling away— falling, falling, falling. You've all had dreams like that; where when you woke your heart was beating because you were falling. Picture in your mind hanging over a precipice—and God is hanging onto you—and you're hanging onto him.*
>
> *And you decide you don't need him anymore. So you let go. But the moment you let go you know you made a mistake. You're falling, and every moment you fall further and further away from the only source of help and truth and love—and you realize you made a mistake and*

you can't get back up—and you fall further and faster and further and faster into spiritual oblivion—and you know you're going the wrong direction—and you'd give anything to go back, but you can't. And you fall, and you fall, and you fall, and you fall…

How long? Forever. And all the while you're falling you're saying, "I'm further now; I'm further. I'm further from the only source of hope, truth, and love."

In Hell there is never the bliss of

Hopeless is the saddest word in the English language.

annihilation. You'd give anything for annihilation, but it's unavailable— only the conscious continuation of emotional anguish, physical anguish, relational anguish, and spiritual anguish … forever.

Restlessness. *"And the smoke of their torment goes up forever and ever, and they have no rest, day or night."* Revelation 14:11a No matter how much pain we have on earth, our bodies will give out eventually. Our bodies will allow us to rest. Our bodies will even force us to rest. Yet in Hell, there will be no relief for the pain. Not one drop of water. Not one aspirin to dull the pain.

Loneliness. Hell will be a place of complete isolation. Sometimes you will hear people say they want to go to Hell because all their friends will be there. That is a lie. There will be no friendship in Hell. There will be no partying. It is a place of solitary confinement. Due to the fact that it is utter darkness, you may not be aware of the identity of anyone else in Hell.

Hopelessness. Bernard Baruch said, "Hopeless is the saddest word in the English language." I think he is right. If you go to a doctor and he tells you that the condition is hopeless, that is very bad news.

The famous Russian author Fyodor Dostoyevsky expressed the heartrending despair of hopelessness when he penned these well-known words:

To live without hope is to cease to live.
Hell is hopelessness.
It is no accident that above the entrance to Dante's
hell is the inscription:
"Leave behind all hope, you who enter here."[33]

Eternal. This is, perhaps, the most tormenting word of all. *"And besides all this, between us and you a great chasm has been fixed, in order that those who would* *pass from here to you may not be able, and none may cross from there to us.*" Luke 16:26 A hundred trillion million years from now, people will still be in agony in Hell.

The Ransom from Hell

Here is the real message of this chapter: you don't have to go to Hell. Your loved ones don't have to go to Hell. God will forgive, redeem, and save anyone who asks. The Bible says that anyone who calls upon the name of the Lord will be saved. (Romans 10:13)

David wrote:

> *O my soul, bless GOD. From head to toe, I'll bless his holy name! O my soul, bless GOD, don't forget a single blessing! He forgives your sins—every one. He heals your diseases—every one. He redeems you from Hell—saves your life! He crowns you with love and mercy—a paradise crown. Psalm 103:1–4 (The Message)*

We will get into this more later, but I can't finish this chapter without saying: God will redeem you from Hell if you will just ask.

It's not too late...

J. Harold Smith preached a revival service once and he notice a young girl was crying during the invitation. She was visibly convicted by the Holy Spirit. With clinched teeth and white-knuckled grip, she refused the offer of salvation. Her parents saw it too. They asked her if she wanted them to go forward with her, but she refused.

As they were driving home, they were in a tragic accident. Their car was knocked off the road and turned upside down. The mother and father were able to climb out, but the daughter was pinned.

Several motorists stopped to help. One was smoking and did not notice a trail of gasoline coming from the car. He flicked his cigarette into that trail of gasoline.

The car burst into flames.

The mother and father tried to pull their daughter out, but the flames were too intense. With flames burning her alive, the parents thought about the service that had just attended and the message they had just heard. They screamed to her, "Call out to Jesus! Ask Him to forgive you! Ask Him to save you!"

The last words of that young, fourteen year-old girl were, "It's too late."

The sad thing is, it wasn't. It is never too late as long as you have breath.

A Letter from Hell

I close with a fictitious story about some fictitious characters, Zach and Josh. They were the best of friends and did everything together. They went to classes together, they played soccer together, and they hung out on weekends.

Zach was a believer, Josh was not.

Zach never shared his faith with his best friend.

One night they went to a party and had a few too many beers. There was a tragic accident. There was a death. There was funeral. I want you to imagine if Josh could have written a letter to his friend Zach, what would that letter have said?[34]

> *Dear Zach,*
>
> *I died today. It's a lot different than I expected. You see, I always thought that dying would bring me to a world that is foggy and hazy, but this place is crystal clear. It is even more real than my life on earth I can think, I can talk. I can even feel.*
>
> *Right after the wreck, I could feel my spirit leaving my body. It was the weirdest thing, Zach. I thought I heard you screaming out to me man, or was I just imagining things? At first I was*

*just standing in line, getting registered
I guess. They asked me for my name.
They said they had to look in this
thing they called the Book of Life. I
guess they couldn't find it though
because the huge angel standing next
to me grabbed me by the arm and
started dragging me away. I was terrified. I had no idea what was going on.
I asked the angel where he was taking
me but he didn't answer. So I asked
him again. He told me that only those
whose names were written in the
Book of Life could enter into Heaven.
The rest would be condemned to Hell
forever. I was scared. The angel threw
me into some kind of lonely cell where
I have been sitting and thinking for a
long, long time.*

*Do you know what I have been
thinking about? I have been thinking
about you. Zach, you're a Christian.
You said so yourself, we talked about
it three different times today, Kelly
brought it up and you laughed it
away. Coach brought it up during
sports and you changed the subject.
It came up right before the wreck
but the question I can't get out of my
mind is this Zach…why haven't you*

78

ever told me about how to become a Christian? I mean you say you're my friend. If you really were you would have told me about this Jesus and I would have escaped this terrible place that I am headed for.

I can feel my heart pounding in my chest. The angels who have been chosen to cast me into Hell are coming down the hallway. I can hear their voices. I have heard of this Hell, Zach, they call it the Lake of Fire. I can't stand it, Zach, I am terrified. The angels are at the door. No, they are coming in and they are pointing at me. No, they are grabbing me and carrying me out of the room. I can already smell the burning sulfur and brimstone. This is it. I am without hope. Closer, closer, closer. I am bursting with fear, they are holding me over the flames. This is it, they have thrown me in fire.

Why Zach? Why didn't you ever tell me about JESUS?

Your friend,
Josh.

CHAPTER 4

Near Death Experiences

*"Death is nothing more than a doorway,
something you walk through."*
- Dr. George Ritchie

According to a 1992 Gallup poll, about 5 percent of Americans have had a Near Death Experience (NDE). One site estimates that every day, 774 Americans have a NDE. The number is probably larger, because many people don't speak about them, especially those who have experiences where they feel they went to Hell before being resuscitated.[35]

Theologians are split in their thinking about the validity of NDEs.

> *Dr. James MacDonald dismisses the idea entirely. He states: [36]Hebrews 9:27 says it is appointed unto man once to die and after this comes judgment. So I don't think we have a Biblical definition of when a person has actually died but I'm going to tell you that anybody who had a "Near Death Experience" didn't die because if they did die they would have been at the judgment. And if they went—wherever they went—they didn't die, not ultimately…they didn't go through*

the valley of the shadow of death. So I think that what a lot of people report as near death experiences is really something similar to the phenom-enon related to being 'near death.' People talk about seeing a light at the end of the tunnel and experiencing peace. A lot of the people who are ex-periencing peace had a lot of suffering (not surprisingly) just moments before as the body is stopping or ceasing its function at some level that there would be some peace or restfulness in that. But I don't put a lot of stock in people who say they went to Heaven, walked around, "I was talking with my Aunt, she said to say 'Hi' to my sister." I think these seem more like dreams to me honestly.

Other theologians do believe in the validity of NDEs. Some have even speculated that Paul had a NDE. In 2 Corinthians 11, Paul writes about the persecution he experienced in preaching the gospel of Christ. Paul writes in vs. 23 that he had been in "**far more labors, in far more imprisonments, beaten times without number, often in danger of death. Five times I received from the Jews thirty-nine lashes. Three times I was beaten with rods, once I was stoned, three times I was shipwrecked, a night and a day I have spent in the deep.**"

It was in this context Paul wrote the following words about his experience of going to Heaven.

*I know a man in Christ who fourteen
years ago was caught up to the third
Heaven. Whether it was in the body or
out of the body I do not know—God
knows. And I know that this man—
whether in the body or apart from the
body I do not know, but God knows—
was caught up to paradise and heard
inexpressible things, things that no
one is permitted to tell. I will boast
about a man like that, but I will not
boast about myself, except about my
weaknesses. Even if I should choose to
boast, I would not be a fool, because
I would be speaking the truth. But I
refrain, so no one will think more of
me than is warranted by what I do or
say, 2 Corinthians 12:2–6 (NIV)*

Most theologians agree Paul is speaking of himself
in this passage. It's actually quite common for some
Bible authors to use the third person to communicate
something that happened to them. In Mark's gospel,
he speaks of an unnamed young man wearing only a
linen cloth who was watching the betrayal and arrest
of Jesus. One of the officers grabbed at "a certain young
man" and caught only the cloth, which ripped off of his
body and the young man ran away naked.

It's implied in the text that Mark is subtly saying, "This is
me. I was there for the whole thing. I saw it happen."[37]

New Testament scholar Frederick C. Grant agrees with this autobiographical interpretation of Marks comment by saying that it was, "the artist's signature in the corner of the painting."[38]

There are other instances where Bible authors refer to themselves in the third person. Four times in John's Gospel, he refers to himself as "the disciple whom Jesus loved." So, when you understand that the mode of writing in that era found it common for people to refer to themselves in the third person—it seems that Paul is telling the Corinthians about something that happened to him.

Some have speculated that Near Death Experiences are caused from the brain having a lack of oxygen while they're being resuscitated. The problem with that theory is that it doesn't explain the reports of NDE's from hospital patients whose EEG traces (measure of brain activity) became completely flat during resuscitation—showing that there was no activity in their brain. If there is no brain activity and the person is "brain dead"—you cannot say that this experience is the cause of any chemical or psychological brain hallucinations.

So that leads us to a very controversial question: "Are near death experiences real?" I cannot answer that question with absolute certainty. But I believe there is some merit to researching these eyewitness accounts and examining them solely through the lens of Scripture – our only source of absolute truth on what happens *After Life*.

Common denominators in near death experiences

Kenneth Ring, a NDE researcher told the New York Times in 1988 that, "Roughly one out of three people who come close to death will have transcendental experiences."

According to researchers, they've found that people typically have two types of NDE's—positive or negative. Let's talk about the positive NDEs of Heaven first.

Near Death Experiences of Heaven

Raymond Moody, author of *Life After Life*, noted that near-death experiences that were positive tended to have the same attributes:

- An out-of-body experience

- A sense of movement through a tunnel

- A great light that is perceived as incredibly powerful

- Greatly enhanced cognition (convinced that they were not in a dream-like state but their thoughts were very clear, rapid, and hyper-lucid)

- An overwhelming feeling of love and "being at home"

- A brief reunion with loved ones

- A sense of being in the most beautiful place, with the most beautiful music

- A review of one's life

- A brief period of instruction

- A border or a point of no return

- Being told something to the effect of "It is not your time."

- Waking up in one's own body

Out of all of these positive experiences these are the characteristics that were remarkably consistent.

Medical doctors writing about this phenomenon have stated they cannot make any judgments about the meaning of such experiences; they can only describe them. They declare that the sheer number and consistency of these accounts indicate they are real. The thousands of accounts are too consistent to be seriously labeled "anecdotal" and therefore of questionable validity and meaning.[39]

My Mother's Experience

When I was growing up, my mother shared a story with me that I would never forget. She told me about a Near Death Experience she had when she was a small child. Hearing her story is what initially sparked a desire to research the validity of NDE's. Let me allow her to tell of her experience in her own words:

When I was 6 years old living in Newport, Tennessee, I went into the hospital to have a tonsillectomy. This was in the late 50's and being a rural hospital, they let my mother carry me into the operating room. Needless to say I was scared to death and so I wrapped my arms and legs around my mom and would not let go. The nurses plied me from my mother's arms and the anesthesiologist immediately applied the mask with the ether as I was screaming. I inhaled too much too quickly and my heart went into cardiac arrest. When that happened I felt electricity going through my body and I found myself floating up to the ceiling in the operating room…I was above everyone looking down onto the scene and watching what they were doing. I could see the doctor working on my body, the nurse on the opposite side of the table, and the anesthesiologist at the head of the table. I could also see my Mother outside the operating room looking in through a small window in the door. I will never forget that look on her face!

I was aware of a bright light, but I always thought it was the operating room light. However, it was behind me as well—as if I was on the ceiling looking down.

So I can assure you that we have a soul or that spiritual side of us that lives on after our bodies are gone, because that day when they administered the ether, my heart stopped.

This experience is typical of most NDEs. A large number of people who have had NDE's describe leaving their physical body—they often watch the events unfold around them and they can see their former body stretched out in front of them.

Pim van Lommel, a Dutch physician and founder of the International Association for Near Death Studies in Holland, conducted an experiment in ten hospitals in which a shelf was placed high up in the operating room with cards displaying random letters and numerals. No one could see these cards without climbing a ladder. Patients who had clinically died in the operating room were then interviewed to see what they experienced. Although only 18 percent of cardiac-arrest patients reported a NDE, a small percentage of people were able to recall seeing the numbers and letters and reported them accurately.[40]

There have also been accounts of people who have been blind since birth and have one of these NDE and later give vivid, detailed, visual descriptions of what they saw and experienced. How does a blind person do that?

Kimberly Clark Sharp, a Seattle social worker, told the International Association for Near Death Studies about her experience in 1995. A woman named Marie was brought to the hospital following a cardiac arrest. Sharp visited her the next day. Marie told her she left her body and floated above the hospital. When Kimberly doubted her story, Marie described a worn dark blue tennis shoe on the ledge outside of a window on the other side of the hospital. Kimberly decided to humor her. When she looked for the shoe, she found it—exactly the way Marie had described it. [41]

The Bible says that Paul was told things that were inexpressible, "*things that no one is permitted to tell.*"

There have been accounts of Christians who said that they were taken off to the side by angels and taught them amazing things they simply can't remember. It's almost as if the angels were told it was not this person's time and the memory of what was taught was erased.

There is no mention that they were not **permitted** to tell—it's that they **cannot.** Many returnees have also said that there aren't enough words in the human vocabulary to express what they experienced.[42]

Dr. Mary Neal is a born-again Christian and an orthopedic surgeon. She shares her medical practice and her love for outdoor adventure with her husband Bill. In 1999 they planned an adventure that took Mary on a spiritual journey few have taken and returned to talk about.

"My husband and I really enjoying kayaking, we enjoy traveling. We speak Spanish. We've traveled internationally a number of times and so for my husband's birthday, I said "Ok this is the year we are gonna to do it. So we went to Chile for a vacation to kayak."

After a week of kayaking, Bill sat out the final day with a sore back. Mary and the rest of their group kayaked through a treacherous stretch of the river. This is the section of river that is very well known for its waterfalls. There are drops of 10 to 20 feet – which for an experienced Kayaker is not a crazy thing. Mary went over the main drop, and as she crested over the drop and as she hit the bottom of the drop, the front end of her kayak became pinned. She was immediately and completely submerged. Mary said, "The volume and force of the water was such that I was absolutely pressed to the front deck of the boat, and I couldn't move my arms even back far enough to reach my spray skirt, let alone push myself out."

Mary was stuck. The only thing she could do was pray.

"I very sincerely asked that God's will be done and I meant it. I didn't say 'Oh please come and save me.' I really meant it. I asked for God's will to be done and at the moment I asked that, I was overcome by a very physical sensation of being held and comforted and reassured that everything was fine. That my husband would be fine, my four young children would be fine, regardless of whether I lived or died, and I believed that Christ was holding me while I was still on the boat and was the one reassuring me."

After several minutes of searching, the group leaders realized Mary was trapped under the falls. They came out on the rocks and they kept trying to get to the boat but the force of the water was such that they just kept being flushed through. They just couldn't get to her. At one point, they recognized that enough time had elapsed that this was really turning into body recovery and not a rescue.

"My body was being sucked over the front deck and so what that meant was when it got to my knees, my knees bent back on themselves and I could feel that. I didn't have pain. I didn't have fear. I didn't have that sense of air hunger. I knew I had been underwater too long to be alive yet I felt more alive than I've ever felt. This was more real than anything I have ever experienced. As my body broke free from my boat, I felt my spirit break free from my body and I rose up and out of the river."

At that moment Mary said she was looking down on the river. She had left her body. Then she was met by a group of heavenly beings.

"They were absolutely overjoyed to see me and greet me and I them. I knew that they had known me and loved me as long as I existed and I knew that I had known them and loved them. I knew that they had been sent by God. They began taking me down this exceptionally beautiful path that was brilliant and they were taking me toward this great dome structure of sorts that not only was exploding with beauty and color but it was exploding with this absolute love of God that was beyond anything I could ever describe or ever truly explain and I could hardly wait. I was absolutely over-whelmed by the sensation of being home. Of being where I belong. Just as quickly, there was this sense of disappointment that descended on every-one and the spirits who had taken me there told me that it wasn't my time and I had more work to do on earth and I had to go back to my body."

> *According to a Barna survey, only 1% of the population thinks they will be sent to Hell after they die.*

After what seemed like hours with her heavenly host, Dr. Neal returned to the river and watched as her friends recovered her body. She had been underwater for over 15 minutes, perhaps as long as 20—certainly longer than medical science can explain her survival. She was flown back to the United States where she slowly recovered from her injuries. Dr. Neal later wrote a book *To Heaven and Back*, where she talks about the reality of how this experience has changed her life.[43]

Near Death Experiences of Hell

According to a Barna survey, only 1% of the population thinks they will be sent to Hell after they die. Jesus disagrees:

> *Enter by the narrow gate. For the gate is wide and the way is easy that leads to destruction, and those who enter by it are many. For the gate is narrow and the way is hard that leads to life, and those who find it are few.*
> *Matthew 7:13–14*

A surgical nurse at a hospital in Phoenix reported, "We have lots of near-death cases there, and almost all of them are the negative kind. You know what I mean— people who wind up in Hell!"[44]

Many of the NDEs align perfectly with what we know in Scripture, although some do not. So the question is, why?

Suppose a professed atheist who is pronounced clinically dead has a NDE that is positive—how do we reconcile that?

The enemy is a deceiver. When he lies, he speaks his native language. (John 8:44) Scripture says in *"for even Satan disguises himself as an angel of light."* 2 Corinthians 11:14

Steven C. Board states that "it is not surprising for old Lucifer to assume that disguise for his name literally means light bearer and his pre-Adamic effulgence was dazzling."[45]

In one NDE, a person was told, "God has never judged you or anyone. There is no Hell and there is no devil." Bottom line: everything spoken in a NDE is not gospel. *"The spiritual person judges all things"* 1 Corinthians 2:15.

In the chapter on Hell, we looked at the story of Maurice Rawlings, M.D., an unbeliever who came to faith after a negative Near Death Experience. This experience taught him that negative NDEs are under-reported because they are so horrific that people block them from their memories. Rawlings' later research indicates that about half of NDEs are negative. For many people, NDE's are far from blissful.

Similar to the heavenly experiences, some people reported seeing their life flash before their eyes and seeing a bright light. There was a key difference in the negative NDEs: they were unable to move towards the light. Instead of feeling like they are floating upwards, they report being pulled downwards—towards a pit inhabited by demons.

Researchers that have examined the reports of those who have had negative NDE's find certain commonalities.

- A feeling of being dragged down into a pit (as opposed to going up into a tunnel)

- A feeling of falling

- Many of them have visions of demonic beings involved

- A darkness that is perceived as being alive or powerful

- Hopelessness and Isolation

- A real physical torment

Let's unpack each of these characteristics with some testimonies from folks who have had negative NDE's. Think about these in light of what we learned the Bible says about Hell.

A feeling of being dragged down into a pit

For some, these experiences begin even while a person is on the threshold of death.

Evelyn Hazell, a London-based art historian, was at one time fighting for her life against meningitis. She said, "I reached a critical stage in the illness and was hovering between life and death. I was involved in an intense and very real struggle for my life" she told *The Telegraph*. "A being was pulling my legs down to infinite depths. I knew without doubt that if I relaxed and gave in I would be dead. I believe this struggle went on for some considerable time and I eventually managed to break away from whatever was pulling me down."

Mrs. Hazel went on to make a full recovery, but she has never forgotten her terrifying ordeal at the very threshold of death. She said, "I do not believe it was a dream or a hallucination…in every way I was lucid.[46]

A feeling of falling into an abyss.

Jane, a woman who fought for her life after a miscarriage said, "It was an awful feeling—like I was going down a big hole and I couldn't get back up. I was going into this big pit. I was going further and further down, and trying to claw my way back up and kept slipping."[47]

A fellow officer in the Texas Army National Guard relayed his uncle's troubling account. In hushed tones, the uncle related, "I was going down a black tunnel, naked, screaming, with lots of other naked, screaming people, and all of us were clawing at the walls of the black tunnel."[48]

Encounters with demonic beings

"A wild orgy of frenzied taunting, screaming and hitting ensued. I fought like a wild man. All the while it was obvious that they were having great fun. It seemed to be, almost, a game for them, with me as the center-piece of their amusement. My pain became their pleasure. They seemed to want to make me hurt by clawing at me and biting me. Whenever I would get one off me, there were five more to replace the one." [49]

A darkness that is penetrating and powerful

Ian McCormack tells of an inky darkness in his NDE, "As I stood there I began to sense that this wasn't just a physical darkness but that there was something else there. I could feel a cold eerie feeling as though something or someone was looking at me—a spiritual darkness. From the darkness I began to hear men's voices screaming at me telling me to 'shut up, that I deserved to be there, that I was in Hell.'"[50]

Dr. Donald Whitaker, a former atheist, claims to have had a NDE as a non-believer in Jesus Christ when he was 17 years old. He had a condition known as acute hemorrhagic necrotic pancreatitis and it was killing him. He claims that as he was dying, he felt as though his body was "fading away" until all of a sudden he sensed a penetrating darkness. He said, "It was so, so dark…it was like the very darkness just penetrated into your very being as I left my body."

Dr. Whitaker goes on to say that even though some people with NDEs talk about seeing a bright light or floating above their body, or feeling warmth and love, he sensed none of that.

He said, "I felt untold terror because I knew that if I ever went all the way, if I slipped all the way, I would never get back."[51]

Hopelessness and Isolation.

Parachute jumping was Mickey Robinson's passion—until the night when everything started to go wrong, and he found himself ablaze from head to foot. "I experienced a deep hopelessness and horror. Separation is hopelessness! Eternal separation is a torment beyond belief. I want you to know there is a place established somewhere that is eternal separation. I was permitted to not only see, but to experience the feeling of what it would be like to be in this eternal separation. And I began to cry out to God."[52]

A real physical torment.

Bill Wise wrote about his Near Death Experience in *23 Minutes in Hell.* "You desperately long for even a few moments of rest, but you never, ever get that privilege. Imagine for a moment how terrible you feel after forty eight hours of no sleep. In Hell you never sleep, rest or find a quiet moment. No rest from the torments, the screams, the fear, the thirst, the lack of breath, the stench, the heat, the hopelessness. You are isolated from contact with any other people."[53]

Hell experiences further complicate matters for religious believers, because they have no discernable relation to what kind of life a person has lived. In other words, being a good person who goes to church is no guarantee that you won't get into a terrible car accident and suddenly find yourself experiencing what feels, in a very real sense, like Hell. As Nancy Evans Bush has seen, "What we think people deserve has nothing to do with whether they have a glorious experience or a terrible one."[54]

Carl Knighton knows what Hell is like because he says he went there after he accidentally overdosed on a drug called Valium.

He says, "Hell is definitely real. Real. Very much real. Like the Bible says, you are in torment."

Carl grew up in a Christian home where he had been taught that Heaven and Hell were real places. Even as a child, he was sensitive to the things of God, but would admit that he had no relationship with Him. After high school, Carl joined the army and married, yet both his marriage and his military career were short lived.

"A platoon leader and squad leader would come to me and say, you're not doing your job and you should be doing better than this. You are not going to make the next rank. So I got really frustrated."

Carl decided it was time to get out of the Army by going AWOL. He hitchhiked to Ohio to see an old friend. He then went on a two-week drug binge. One night Carl went to a crack house in the worst part of Columbus, Ohio.

"You could smell the stench of the crack cocaine, smell the stench of the marijuana. People was high, laying all across the floors."

Carl smoked some crack and started drinking alcohol and using other drugs. But he says he believes it was the last pill he took that sent him on a journey to Hell.

"I took that Valium and before I knew it, I fell off the couch onto the floor. It was pitch black, dark. I began to quiver, I began to have the shakes, and I began to go down and down and down like a deep pit and I saw and smelled the stench of Hell. It's the most rottenness thing that you can ever smell in your life. In fact, you can't even imagine it. I began to feel a tugging, a pulling like the Bible said demons tug and nag at you. They were calling my name. 'You belong to us now.' I saw souls, lost souls that were in torment in the lake of fire. They were crying and calling on God..."

Carl said that when he came back to his body "I was shaking and trembling and I turned my head to the right and they said I was dead and they said I was dead for 30 to 35 minutes."

Three days later Carl returned to Fort Eustis, Virginia to face the consequences of going AWOL. He was demoted and confined to the barracks for one month. During that time alone, he completely surrendered his life to Jesus Christ.

Carl said, "He loved me so much that he gives me a second chance and I'm here to tell the story…don't throw your life away. Accept Jesus as your Savior."[55]

Near Death Experiences change people

According to the International Association of Near Death (IAND), about 80 percent of those who have had a NDE claim their lives were forever changed. A pattern of surprising dimensions emerged. These individuals didn't return just with a renewed zest for life and a more spiritual outlook; they showed specific psychological and physiological differences on a scale never before faced by them. This is as true with children as it is with teenagers and adults.

Here are a few of the aftereffects as reported from various studies:

- They no longer feared death.

- Some went through serious bouts of depression because they couldn't stay in Heaven.

- They became more generous and charitable than they had been before their experience.

- Afterward, they initiated and maintained more satisfying relationships.

- Unresolved issues from childhood tended to resurface in their lives.

- They became less competitive, faced less stress and enjoyed life more.

- They became convinced that their lives had a purpose.

- Many spoke of loving and accepting others more readily.

- Their shift in behavior often confused (and threatened) family members, especially when a formerly aloof, uncaring individual became loving and thoughtful.

- Marriages sometimes failed because of the dramatic personality shift of the person who had the experience.

- After a near-death experience, individuals tended to be more aware of the present moment—of living in the now. They weren't disposed to make future plans.

- They used the language of place freely. They spoke of "going there" and "coming back." They often described the beauty of trees, grass and flowers. They raved about the quality of the light and the fragrances that were new to them.

- They believed that what happened to them was real.

Responding to such aftereffects takes time. Research indicates that the first three years tend to be the most confusing for people, almost as if they still have not fully returned.[56]

Near Death Experiences are too common to ignore. A Near Death Experience is just that—an *experience*. If someone has an experience that contradicts Scripture, we should always go with Scripture.

Studying the topic of NDE's provide an interesting and controversial window in what could potentially lie in store for all mankind in that moment of death. They offer further evidence that we are eternal beings who should concern ourselves with what happens after life.

CHAPTER 5

The Rewards of Eternity

*""Rejoice and be glad, for your reward
in heaven is great..."*
- Matthew 5:12

Salvation is given to us by grace through faith. Rewards, on the other hand, are given on the basis of works. Jesus said, *"Blessed are you when people hate you and when they exclude you and revile you and spurn your name as evil, on account of the Son of Man! Rejoice in that day, and leap for joy, for behold, your reward is great in Heaven; for so their fathers did to the prophets"* (Luke 6:22–23).

Notice He gives us a reason to rejoice in persecution: because of reward. There is a direct connection between deeds done for Christ on earth and a great reward in Heaven. This is not an isolated teaching on the part of Jesus. He talked about it all the time. We receive a gift for believing: eternal life. We receive rewards for doing. Here are some other verses that speak to this:

- *For the Son of Man is going to come in His Father's glory with his angels, and then He will reward each person according to what they have done.* Matthew 16:27 (NIV)

- *Jesus said to him, "If you would be perfect, go, sell what you possess and give to the poor, and you*

103

will have treasure in Heaven; and come, follow me." Matthew 19:21

- *You will be blessed, because they cannot repay you. For you will be repaid at the resurrection of the just.* Luke 14:14

There are two keys that determine everything about your eternity. The first key is your faith. That unlocks the door to eternal life. We are not saved by trying. We are saved by trusting.

The second key is behavior. That opens the door to reward. Faith determines where you will spend eternity. Works determine how you will spend eternity—whether you will have a great or small reward.

Imagine a friend who built a rocket to go to the nearest star to our solar system, Proxima Centauri. It is 4.2 light years away. Using an Ion Drive Propulsion system, it would take 81,000 years. Imagine the absence of Earth's gravity caused the aging process to magically stop. Hang with me.

Your friend decides to give you a tour of his rocket. There are two parts. The first part will be burned up during lift off. The second, much smaller part, would travel the 4.2 light-year trip. Which part do you think he should decorate? Which part should have the big screen TV?

You would immediately see that no matter how cramped and uncomfortable that first part was, it was the second part that mattered.

Jesus saw the wisdom in this kind of thinking. *"Do not lay up for yourselves treasures on earth, where moth and rust destroy and where thieves break in and steal, but lay up for yourselves treasures in Heaven, where neither moth nor rust destroys and where thieves do not break in and steal."* Matthew 6:19–20

Here is the big idea of this chapter: eternity lasts a long, long time.

What happens on the dot called today has ramifications for the line called eternity. The things we do today send ripples into eternity. Today matters for forever.

One more word picture, imagine a chain that goes

> *Salvation is given to us by grace through faith. Rewards, on the other hand, are given on the basis of works.*

from here to that same star, Proxima Centauri. This life is one link of the chain. What you do during this life affects the whole chain. Today matters. It matters for all eternity. No good deed will go unrewarded.

What you believe in this life determines where you spend eternity. How you behave in this life determines how you spend eternity.

The two judgments

In the movie *The Truman Show*, Jim Carrey plays the role Truman Burbank who is secretly being observed by five thousand cameras. He doesn't know it, but every move he makes is being observed by an audience of millions. It makes for good drama and illustrates the point I want to make in this section: your life is on camera. Like Truman Burbank, every move you make is being observed. Truman Burbank had an unseen audience and so do we.

Bette Midler had it right when she sang, "God is watching us. God is watching us." She got it wrong in the last line, "God is watching us, from a distance." He isn't watching from a distance. He is watching up close and personal.

Hebrews 4:13 says, ***"And no creature is hidden from His sight, but all are naked and exposed to the eyes of Him to whom we must give account."*** He is the God who sees. He sees everything. And eventually, we will stand before Him and explain everything we have done.

The Bible teaches that everyone—lost and saved alike—will live for eternity. There are six main events of all of our life:

1.   We are born.

2. We die.

3. We go to a temporary Heaven or Hell.

4. The resurrection. The Bible teaches that both the lost and the saved will experience a resurrection. We will all be given a new body.

5. The judgment. The saved will stand before the Judgment Seat of Christ. The lost will experience the Great White Throne Judgment.

6. Eternity in the final Heaven or Hell.

Let's talk about the Great White Throne Judgment first. Scripture teaches that only unbelievers will be at this judgment. Its purpose is the judgment of sin.

> *Then I saw a great white throne and him who was seated on it. From his presence earth and sky fled away, and no place was found for them. And I saw the dead, great and small, standing before the throne, and books were opened. Then another book was opened, which is the book of life. And the dead were judged by what was written in the books, according to what they had done. And the sea gave up the dead who were in it, Death and Hades gave up the dead who were in them, and they were judged, each one of them, according to what they had done. Then Death*

*and Hades were thrown into the lake
of fire. This is the second death, the
lake of fire. And if anyone's name was
not found written in the book of life,
he was thrown into the lake of fire.*
- **Revelation 20:11–15**

Everyone whose name is not written in the Lamb's Book of Life will face God at this judgment. The Lamb's Book of Life includes the names of every person who has believed in God and trusted Him for their salvation. One by one, unbelievers will come forward. One by one, they will give their name. One by one, they will see that their name is not written in the Lamb's Book of Life. One by one, they will face eternity in Hell.

These are the same people who refused to repent. These are the people who refused to believe. These are the people who refused to bend the knee. Eventually, everyone will bend the knee.

These are the people who claim their life is good enough. Imagine what happens next is like a big movie screen. Someone claims they have been good enough and do not, deserve to go to Hell. Jesus doesn't say anything, He just starts the movie. Every selfish act, every sexual sin, every act of greed—it's all there.

But, let me emphasize the point: The Great White Throne Judgment is only for the non-believer.

The second judgment is The Judgment Seat of Christ. This is for believers. Its purpose is for the judgment of service. Your eternal destination is not determined at

The Judgment Seat of Christ. That was already determined here on this earth when you choose to receive and believe. (John 1:12)

We will not be judged at The Great White Throne Judgment because we have already been judged. Jesus took our judgment on the cross. *"There is therefore now no condemnation for those who are in Christ Jesus."* Romans 8:1

We don't have to be judged because Jesus was already judged in our place. When we receive Him, our names are written in the Lamb's Book of Life.

But, there is a judgment for believers, that has to do with reward. Romans 14:10b says, *"We will all stand before the judgment seat of God."* And in 2 Corinthians 5:10 we read, *"For we must all appear before the judgment seat of Christ, so that each one may receive what is due for what he has done in the body, whether good or evil."*

The Greek word for *judgment seat* is *bema. Bema* means *a step up.* The bema seat was used in the Olympic Games. When an athlete wins a competition they step up onto the bema seat. The judge comes and puts a crown on their head.

This is the imagery that Paul is using here. In Heaven there will be degrees of reward. Every good deed will be observed and every good deed will be rewarded.

This same is true of Hell. Every bad deed will be observed and every bad deed will be punished. For Adolf

Hitler, who was responsible for the death of millions of Jews, the punishment of Hell will be far more severe than for Joe Six-pack.

Here are four passages that speak to degrees of punishment in Hell.

In Matthew 11:20–24 Jesus compares the judgment that awaits those who personally heard Him with famous sinners in the past. He says it will be far worse for those who personally heard Him and rejected than for those who had not heard Him. *"But I tell you, it will be more bearable on the day of judgment for Tyre and Sidon than for you. And you, Capernaum, will you be exalted to Heaven? You will be brought down to Hades. For if the mighty works done in you had been done in Sodom, it would have remained until this day."* Matthew 11:22–23

The principle is this: we are all responsible for the light we have been given. Those who have had the opportunity to know of Christ and reject Him will be judged more severely than those who never knew of Christ.

In Luke 12 Jesus spells this out, *"And that servant who knew his master's will but did not get ready or act according to his will, will receive a severe beating. But the one who did not know, and did what deserved a beating, will receive a light beating. Everyone to whom much was given, of him much will be required, and from him to whom they entrusted much, they will demand the more"* (Luke 12:47–48).

Notice the mention of a "light beating" and "many blows." This clearly indicates that there will be degrees of punishment in Hell. R.C. Sproul said, "However, not all sins are equally bad. To murder someone is far worse than to hate the person, even though both sins fall under the same category. Committing adultery in the flesh is more heinous than committing adultery in the heart, though both are condemned."[57]

In John 19 we read of a conversation at one of Jesus's trials:

> So Pilate said to him, "You will not
> speak to me? Do you not know
> that I have authority to release you
> and authority to crucify you?" Jesus
> answered him, "You would have no
> authority over me at all unless it had
> been given you from above. Therefore
> he who delivered me over to you has
> the greater sin." John 19:10–11

Note the reference to greater sin. Greater sin demands greater punishment. Any sin will separate you from God. But, all sins are not equally bad and will not be punished equally. Elmer Towns makes this clear:[58]

> It was a great sin for Pilate to allow
> Jesus to be crucified, but the religious
> leaders and Judas, who delivered
> Jesus to death, committed a greater
> sin than Pilate.

Even the law in the Old Testament recognizes the difference between murder and manslaughter. Manslaughter was a person unintentionally killing another. But murder was premeditated and intentional.

One more. Notice the reference to **worse punishment in** Hebrews 10:

Anyone who has set aside the law of Moses dies without mercy on the evidence of two or three witnesses. How much worse punishment, do you think, will be deserved by the one who has trampled underfoot the Son of God, and has profaned the blood of the covenant by which he was sanctified, and has outraged the Spirit of grace? Hebrews 10:28–29

It is clear from these passages that God is a just judge. Those who sin worse will be judged more severely. Those whose sin is lighter will receive a lighter punishment. This leaves just one more question.

How To Increase Your Rewards In Heaven

Jesus offers some great financial advice in the Sermon on the Mount:

"Do not lay up for yourselves treasures on earth, where moth and rust destroy and where thieves break in and steal, but lay up for yourselves treasures in Heaven, where neither moth nor rust destroys and where thieves do not break in and steal. For where your treasure is, there your heart will be also." - **Matthew 6:19–21**

There is nothing wrong with storing up treasure on earth. However, far better to store up treasures in Heaven.

Jesus' teaching reminds me of that commercial where a man asks children, "Which is better, bigger or smaller?" Jesus is asking, "Which is better, a safe investment with a big reward or a risky investment with a poor reward?" Investing in Heaven is a safe investment with a big reward.

Notice that storing up treasures is not discouraged. Storing up treasures where they can be lost is discouraged. Storing up treasures where they will be safe is commanded.

Financial advisors will tell you to take a long time-perspective. It is better to invest with a twenty-year perspective than a two-year perspective. Jesus says to invest with a twenty-million-year perspective.

Notice the appeal to self-interest. The appeal of the gospel is always to deny yourself, in the short run, in order to receive the greater benefit in the long run. In a way, it is an appeal to your self-interest. It is always in our best interest to live the Christian life.

Whenever someone dies, someone enviably asks the question, "What did he leave behind?" Answer: "All of it."

You have never seen a U-Haul behind a hearse. The Egyptian pharaohs tried it. That is what those massive pyramids are all about. "To properly care for his spirit, the corpse was mummified, and everything the king would need in the afterlife was buried with him, including gold vessels, food, furniture and other offerings."[59] It doesn't work that way.

Let's look at what the Bible says.

> For no one can lay a foundation other
> than that which is laid, which is Jesus
> Christ. Now if anyone builds on the
> foundation with gold, silver, precious
> stones, wood, hay, straw—each one's
> work will become manifest, for the
> Day will disclose it, because it will be
> revealed by fire, and the fire will test
> what sort of work each one has done.
> If the work that anyone has built
> on the foundation survives, he will
> receive a reward. If anyone's work is
> burned up, he will suffer loss, though
> he himself will be saved, but only as
> through fire. 1 Corinthians 3:11–15

Every day you are building something. We have two types of building materials we can use:

- Bricks
- Sticks

Every day you ought to ask yourself: will this make it through the fire? We know two things will make it through the fire:

- The Word of God
- The People of God

Invest your life in these two things that will make it through the fire. Acquiring more stuff will not make it through the fire. The Word of God and the people of God will. The Bible says, *"The grass withers, the flower fades, but the word of our God will stand forever."* Isaiah 40:8

There is nothing wrong with storing up treasure on earth. However, far better to store up treasures in Heaven.

Examine Your Life

Jesus said, *"For where your treasure is, there your heart will be also."* Matthew 6:21

What are you investing into sticks, and what are you investing into bricks?

People do all kind of things with their sticks. Sticks are not bad. We all need some sticks. The Bible says, *"But if we have food and clothing, with these we will be content."* 1 Timothy 6:8 We all need food and clothing. But the excessive attention to sticks is foolish. Don't get too attached to your sticks.

Many people focus only on their sticks. They love their sticks. They protect their sticks. They build luxurious homes with their sticks. They put wheels on their sticks. They will take their sticks to the lake and put them on a boat. They hit little white balls with their very expensive sticks. They insure their sticks so that they cannot lose their sticks. But they *can* lose their sticks. Eventually, everyone will lose their sticks. Sticks don't make it through the fire. That is why Jesus said not to focus our lives on sticks.

Examine yourself. Are you living your life for bricks or sticks? Have you done anything in the last seven days that is going to make it through the fire?

What does it mean to live your life for bricks? Here is one church that did:[60]

Just two years ago he was the town drunk. He drank away his first marriage and came within a prayer of doing the same with the second. He and his wife were so consumed with alcohol that they farmed out their kids to neighbors and resigned themselves to a drunken demise.

But then someone saw them. Members of an area church took a good look at their situation. They began bringing the couple food and clothing. They invited them to attend worship services. Bzuneh was not interested. However, his wife, Bililie, was. She began to sober up and consider the story of Christ. The promise of a new life. The offer of a second chance. She believed.

Bzuneh was not so quick. He kept drinking until one night a year later he fell so hard he knocked a dent in his face that remains to this day. Friends found him in a gully and took him to the same church and shared the same Jesus with him. He hasn't touched a drop since.

It all began with an honest look and a helping hand. Could this be God's strategy for human hurt? First, kind eyes meet desperate ones. Next, strong hands help weak ones. Then, the miracle of God. We do our small part, he does the big part.

Exchange Your Currency

Exchanging your currency from sticks to bricks has to do with two things:

- Time

- Money

When you invest your time into people and serving others, you are storing up treasures in Heaven. When you teach children in a Sunday School class, you are storing up treasure in Heaven. When you spend time in the Word, you are investing in one of the two things that will make it through the fire. When you serve the poor, you are investing in Heaven.

In addition to our time, we need to invest our treasure. God doesn't need our money. He wants what our money represents—our hearts. If God is not first place in my money, He is not first place in my life. The Bible says that where your treasure is, there you heart will be as well.

Sometimes people tell me they love Jesus but they never give anything to Kingdom Work. It is a lie. Jesus said it is not so. If you do not give to Jesus' work, you do not love Jesus. If you want to love God more deeply, invest in Kingdom Work more heavily. Your heart will follow your money.

Do you care how Wal-Mart's stock is doing? If you are invested in Wal-Mart, you do. If you are not invested in Wal-Mart, you don't. Your heart follows your investment.

Your calendar and your checkbook reveal what is on your heart.

Express Your Faith

God will reward you for the level of devotion that you seek Him. When we spend time seeking to know and experience more of His presence in our lives through spiritual acts such as fasting, praying and spending time in the Word—God promises to reward us in eternity for that. Jesus said, *"But when you pray, go into your room and shut the door and pray to your Father who is in secret. And your Father who sees in secret will reward you."* Matthew 6:6

God will reward people who make spiritual disciplines a priority. Godly people are in the habit of starting their day with their Bibles on their laps. They follow the example of Jesus, *"And rising very early in the morning, while it was still dark, he departed and went out to a desolate place, and there he prayed."* Mark 1:35

God will reward you for hard work. *"Whatever you do, work heartily, as for the Lord and not for men,* *knowing that from the Lord you will receive the inher-itance as your reward. You are serving the Lord Christ."* Colossians 3:23–24

Are you working as if your boss were Jesus? If you do, you will be rewarded. He notices when you are on time or late. He notices the length of your breaks. He notices what time you take off.

If you are feeling condemned about now, let me remind you, *"There is therefore now no condemnation for those who are in Christ Jesus."* Romans 8:1 Condemnation has no place in the Christian life. No place. This is not about being condemned, it is about reward.

Nothing you could do could make God love you more. Nothing you could do could make God love you less. You could not work so badly that God would condemn you. But, if you work hard, He will richly reward you.

God will reward you for loving those who are hard to love. Jesus said, *"For if you love those who love you, what reward do you have? Do not even the tax collectors do the same?"* Matthew 5:46 The implication of this verse is that if you do love those who don't love you, you will be rewarded. If you love those who are hard to love, you will be rewarded.

Every church has people who are hard to love. Love them anyway. Every family has people who are hard to love. Love them anyway. There is a reward for those who do.

God will reward you for serving others in His name. Jesus said, *"And whoever gives one of these little ones even a cup of cold water because he is a disciple, truly, I say to you, he will by no means lose his reward."* Matthew 10:42 The cup of cold water is symbolic of a small act of service. We might think that God would not notice a small act of service. You will hear people say, "It was nothing." It may not be much, but God notices and will reward every act of service, small and large.

In the story of the talents, Jesus had the one-talent man who did not use what he had been given. I think it is significant that the one-talent man did not serve. He probably felt he only had one talent, what could he do? Whatever talent you have been given, serve the Lord with all of your heart. You will be rewarded.

God will reward acts of hospitality. *"The one who receives a prophet because he is a prophet will receive a prophet's reward, and the one who receives a righteous person because he is a righteous person will receive a righteous person's reward."* Matthew 10:41 *Receive* in this context means to offer hospitality. One commentary explains it this way:[61]

> *Much of the evangelistic and teaching ministry of the early church was performed by traveling missionaries who served the various churches and were dependent on the hospitality and gifts of the members of the churches they visited. One striking example is*

Gaius, who was especially faithful in exercising hospitality (3 John 6); many traveling missionaries shared with John's church how generous Gaius had been. John commends Gaius for his hospitality.

The Bible has much to say about hospitality. The Christian faith is a faith of hospitality. There is something about breaking bread in the home of a brother that builds fellowship. Consider these key verses on hospitality:

- *Seek to show hospitality*. Romans 12:13

- *Show hospitality to one another without grumbling*. 1 Peter 4:9

- *Dear friend, when you extend hospitality to Christian brothers and sisters, even when they are strangers, you make the faith visible.* 3 John 5 (The Message)

Do you enjoy having guests into your home? It is almost a forgotten art. But, it will not be forgotten by God. Every act of hospitality will be rewarded in Heaven.

One more thing. When you have people over, invite people who are not a part of your group. Don't just invite your family and your people. Jesus told us who to invite for maximum reward:

He said also to the man who had invited him, "When you give a dinner or a banquet, do not invite your friends or your brothers or your relatives or rich neighbors, lest they also invite you in return and you be repaid. But when you give a feast, invite the poor, the crippled, the lame, the blind, and you will be blessed, because they cannot repay you. For you will be repaid at the resurrection of the just." Luke 14:12–14

God will reward you for suffering without losing your faith. *"Blessed are you when others revile you and persecute you and utter all kinds of evil against you falsely on my account. Rejoice and be glad, for your reward is great in Heaven, for so they persecuted the prophets who were before you."* Matthew 5:11–12

Have you ever been made fun of for being a Christian? You will be rewarded. Have you ever been criticized because you would not do that? You will be rewarded. Have you ever been mocked because you would not go there? You will be rewarded.

God will reward you for the giving that no one sees. *"Thus, when you give to the needy, sound no trumpet before you, as the hypocrites do in the synagogues and in the streets, that they may be praised by others. Truly, I say to you, they have received their reward. But when you give to the needy, do not let your left hand know what your right hand is doing, so that* *your giving may be in secret. And your Father who sees in secret will reward you."* Matthew 6:2–4

Notice again the appeal to self-interest. John Piper says,[62]

> *In other words, stop being motivated by the praises of men, and let the thought of God's reward move you to love.*
>
> *Yes, it is real love when our giving is motivated by the Heavenly treasure. It is not exploitation, because the loving almsgiver aims for His alms to rescue the beggar for that same reward. A Christian…is always aware that his own enjoyment of the Father's reward will be even greater when shared with the ones He has drawn into the Heavenly fellowship.*

What About Crowns?

Let's look at the five crowns that the Bible says we will be rewarded with in Heaven. There may be more, but the Bible mentions at least five.

The incorruptible crown. Paul compares Christian living to an athletic completion:

> *Do you not know that in a race all the runners run, but only one gets the prize? Run in such a way as to get the prize. Everyone who competes in the games goes into strict training. They do it to get a crown that will not last, but we do it to get a crown that will last forever. Therefore I do not run like someone running aimlessly; I do not fight like a boxer beating the air. No, I strike a blow to my body and make it my slave so that after I have preached to others, I myself will not be disqualified for the prize. 1 Corinthians 9:24–27 (NIV)*

The word translated *crown* here could be translated "wreath." It was a wreath that would not last.[63] Corinth itself hosted major games for all of Greece every two years on the isthmus; these were the best-attended Greek festivals next to the Olympic games, which were held every four years.

The flowers the athletes received were like flowers on Valentine's Day—nice, but temporary. Our future crown though is like a gold ring—beautiful, valuable, and lasting.

How do we receive this incorruptible crown? Paul gives the answer: **strict training**. Suppose you got up tomorrow and decided to run a marathon—which is 26 grueling miles. How would you do? What if you tried really hard?

I'm not a runner. The other day I tried to go for a run but then I stopped because I forgot something – I forgot that I was too out of shape and I can't run!

However, suppose I got up tomorrow and started training. What if I would run and walk for thirty minutes a day every day – eventually working up to an hour a day. Once a week I run farther—perhaps three or four hours. Suppose I did this for an entire year. What are my odds now? Certainly much better.

John Ortberg says that Christian living is not so much about trying hard as training well. It is not about trying hard to be loving and kind and selfless. It is not about trying not to worry. It is about what Paul says here—going into strict training.

It is about spending time in the Word on a disciplined basis. It is about memorizing and meditating on the Word of God until our thinking is changed. It is about being transformed by the renewing of your mind.

Participating in strict training will yield an incorruptible crown.

The crown of righteousness. *"Now there is in store for me the crown of righteousness, which the Lord, the righteous Judge, will award to me on that day—and not only to me, but also to all who have longed for his appearing."* 2 Timothy 4:8 (NIV)

There is a sense in which we have been saved, are being saved, and will be saved. Similarly, there is a sense in which we have already been made righteous. There is a sense in which we have already received the crown of righteousness. This is why Christ died, to make us righteous. *"For our sake he made him to be sin who knew no sin, so that in him we might become the righteousness of God."* 2 Corinthians 5:21

But we live in the tension between the now and the not yet. Someday we will receive the crown of righteousness. As Gordon Fee aptly remarks, "One receives the final crown of righteousness precisely because one has already received the righteousness of Christ."[64]

How do we receive this crown of righteousness? By longing for Christ's returning. By being unhappy with this life and longing for the next. Imagine a child just days before Christmas. He can't wait to open those presents. That is how we are to long to be with Jesus in Heaven.

The crown of rejoicing. *"For what is our hope or joy or crown of boasting before our Lord Jesus at his coming? Is it not you? For you are our glory and joy."* 1 Thessalonians 2:19–20

This is sometimes called the soul-winners crown. It has to do with the joy that comes to those who have a part in bringing others to Christ. "Every believer is not called to preach, but everyone is called to sow the precious seed of God's Word and to be constantly seeking to win others to Christ. Great will be our rejoicing in Heaven when we see those who have been led to salvation through our testimony and the patient teaching of God's Word."[65]

The crown of glory. *"So I exhort the elders among you, as a fellow elder and a witness of the sufferings of Christ, as well as a partaker in the glory that is going to be revealed: shepherd the flock of God that is among you, exercising oversight, not under compulsion, but willingly, as God would have you; not for shameful gain, but eagerly; not domineering over those in your charge, but being examples to the flock. And when the chief Shepherd appears, you will receive the unfading crown of glory."* 1 Peter 5:1–4

> *Some are working for a Ph.D., or an Ed.D., or an M.D. degree. I am working for a W.D. — Well done!*

This is the crown for those who are ministering to or caring for other people. It is sometimes called a pastor's crown or a shepherd's crown, but it is not a crown just for pastors. This is a crown for anyone who gives spiritual direction or care for other people. It might be given to those who serve as a small group leader or Bible Study leader. Anyone who helps to shepherd God's flock will receive this crown.

The Crown of Life. *"Blessed is the man who remains steadfast under trial, for when he has stood the test he will receive the crown of life, which God has promised to those who love him."* James 1:12

This is the crown given to those who endure intense trials. Have you noticed that life is hard? Hang in there. You will be rewarded, along with Henry Morrison.

Henry Morrison was a missionary in Africa for forty years. Upon his retirement, he sent letters to his sponsoring church to let them know the details of when he was coming home. As he entered the harbor, he could not believe his eyes. There were crowds of people there to welcome him. They held up a big banner that said, "Welcome Home!" There was cheering and waving and yelling and laughter and joy. There was a big band playing triumphant music. Words cannot describe his joy.

He went down stairs to get his luggage. This took a little longer than he anticipated, and when he came outside, the band was gone. The crowd had dissipated. The dock was practically silent.

He asked who the welcome party was for.

"Didn't you know? President Teddy Roosevelt was on this ship. He had been on a hunting expedition in Africa and the welcome home celebration was for him.

Henry Morrison and his wife found a park bench and sat down. He started to feel sorry for himself. He began to weep. He said, "I just don't get it. The President of the United States goes on a hunting expedition in Africa and he gets a welcome home party. We spent forty years serving Jesus in Africa and no one comes to welcome us home."

His wife wisely responded, "Henry, we are not home yet."

Some are working for a Ph.D., or an Ed.D., or an M.D. degree. I am working for a W.D. —Well done!

*"**His master said to him, 'Well done, good and faithful servant. You have been faithful over a little; I will set you over much. Enter into the joy of your master.**'"* Matthew 25:23

CHAPTER 6

How Can You Be Sure You Have Eternal L.I.F.E.?

Jesus said, "I came that they may have life, and have it abundantly."
- John 10:10

I would not want to close this book without first telling you how you can experience an abundant life here on earth and an eternal life with God in Heaven. I simply want to ask you to reflect on two questions that I believe will be the most important questions you need to answer in this life.

First, are you 100% sure that if you were to die today you would go to Heaven?

You may be thinking, "Well, I would probably have to say that I am 50% sure or maybe even 90%. But the Word of God tells us in I John 5:13, "*These things I have written to you who believe in the name of the Son of God so that you might know that you have eternal life*." God doesn't want you to have a "hope-so" salvation but a "know-so" salvation. God does not want you to be a doubting Christian; He wants you to be a shouting Christian! You can't tell me that you are content with a "90% assurance" when your eternal destiny weighs in the balance! You need to be completely sure of it and God's Word teaches that you can be. Dwight L. Moody once said, "I have never met anybody who was any

131

good to the service of Christ who first of all did not have assurance of his or her salvation."

Secondly, if you were to meet Christ face-to-face and He were to ask you "Why should I let you into Heaven?" what do you think you would say?

Basically, there are three answers that people will give in response to this question.

The Answer of Behavior. You might say, "Well I'm a good person. I try to live a moral life." If you have this kind of mindset, you think that if the good you have done outweighs the bad, then someday when you get to Heaven, if the scales tip in your favor, God will let you in. Friend, this is one of the greatest lies that Satan feeds to people. If you could be a good, moral person and still make it into Heaven, why would Jesus have to die for your sins. Ephesians 2:8-9 says, "*For by grace you have been saved through faith; and that not of yourselves, it is the gift of God; not as a result of works, so that no one may boast*."

The Answer of Birth: How many times have you heard people say, "I've been a Christian ALL my life"? If you are this person, as sincere as you might be, you have missed what it means to truly be a Christian. Christianity is not something you are humanly born into. Being born into a Christian home doesn't make you a Christian any more than being born in a hospital makes you a doctor!

The Answer of Belief. There is only one door to Heaven. It is not the back door of behavior; it is not the side door of birth; it is the front door of belief. In John 14:6, *"Jesus answered, I am the way and the truth and the life, no man cometh unto the Father but by me!"* The only answer to man's problem, to your problem, is to believe in the Lord Jesus Christ.

Most people make the mistake of thinking that church is all about religion. God hates man's religion. What separates Christianity from Islam, Buddhism, Hinduism and all other world beliefs is that they all are attempts to reach upward to God. Christianity is the only religion that has God reaching down to man. There is a big difference between man's religion and the gospel of Jesus Christ.

Are you 100% sure that if you were to die today you would go to Heaven?

- Religion says, "Try," but the gospel says, "trust."

- Religion says, "Pay me what you owe." The gospel says, "I'll pay what you owe."

- Religion says, "Live for God." The gospel says, "Live through God."

- Religion says, "Obey the law," but the gospel says, "Obey the Lord."

- Religion says "Do," but the gospel says, "Done."

- Religion says, "Attain righteousness." The gospel says, "Accept righteousness."

- Religion says, "My way is the right way." The gospel says, "God's way is the only way."

- Religion says "Salvation is in a formula." The gospel says, "Salvation is by faith."

- Religion says "Believe something," but the gospel says, "Receive someone!"

You don't need dead rituals or dry religion. What you need is a Divine Redeemer, and His name is Jesus Christ!

Jesus said in John 10:10, *"I have come that you might have life and have it more abundantly."* The best way that I know to explain to you how you can have this kind of relationship with God is by using the acronym L.I.F.E.

Love

God made man to love Him forever. The Bible says in John 3:16, *"For God so loved the world that He gave His one and only son, so that whosoever should believe in Him, would not perish but have eternal life."* God created you to live in a relationship with Him. God wants to offer you hope, peace, and a purpose for why you are here on this earth. The best news, I could ever tell you is that God has a wonderful plan for your life. He loves you and desires for you to be in a right relationship with Him. Romans 5:8 says, *"But God demonstrates His own love toward us in that while we were yet sinners, Christ died for us."* God loves you so much that He would send His Son to die for you. Even if you were the only person on the face of this earth, Jesus Christ still would have died for you. You are special to Him.

But if God loves you and desires a relationship with you, then why is it that you feel so isolated from Him? That brings me to the next point…

Isolation

Sin, the wrong things that you and I have done, is what isolates us from God. It builds a wall that separates humanity from God. Sin is rebellion against God and keeps us from experiencing eternal life in Heaven and abundant life on earth.

Here are two basic facts about sin:

All of us have sinned. The Bible says in Romans 3:23, *"For all have sinned and fall short of the glory of God."* There is not a single person reading this book who has lived a perfect life, and that is why we need a perfect Savior.

Sin is the cause of physical and spiritual death. Romans 6:23 says, *"For the wages of sin is death."* If you were to take all the nuclear weapons in the world, strap them to your body and detonate them, it would vaporize your body in a nanosecond, but it wouldn't take away the sin that is in your soul. Only the blood of Jesus Christ can blow sin out of a man's heart. Only the blood of Jesus Christ can cleanse us and make us pure and make us clean.

I would be cruel if I did not warn you that Hell is a reality. God has never sent a single person to Hell. People send themselves to Hell by not accepting His free gift of eternal life.

So how can you get past this isolation and experience a relationship with Jesus Christ. God wants to offer you His forgiveness...

Forgiveness

Forgiveness is the only solution to the isolation problem.

The only way that our relationship can be restored with God is for our sins to be forgiven. Jesus Christ died on the cross for that very purpose. I Peter 3:18 says, "*Jesus died for all sins once for everyone... to bring you to God.*" His death made it possible to be forgiven but you have to ask for it.

Eternal Life

Eternal life and a one-on-one relationship with God can be a reality for you now and forever. John 1:12 says, "*Yet to all who have received Him* (Jesus) *to those who have believed in His name, He gave the right to become children of God."*

The ability to have the life that you've always dreamed about is right within your grasp. Do you want that life today—an abundant life on earth and eternal life in Heaven? It's as easy as A.B.C.

Admit you are a sinner and that you are willing to make a 180-degree turn from your sin. That's what it means to repent. Acts 3:19 says, *"Repent, then, and turn to God, so that your sins may be wiped out."*

Believe that Jesus died for your sins and rose again from the dead.

Forgiveness is the only solution to the isolation problem.

Confess verbally and publicly your belief in Jesus Christ. *"That if you confess with your mouth 'Jesus is Lord,' and believe in your heart that God raised Him from the dead, you will be saved."* (Romans 10:9, 10)

Life's greatest discovery is that you can go to Heaven by faith in the Lord Jesus Christ. You don't have to pay for your sins—Jesus has already paid. You don't have to die in your sins—Jesus has already died. You don't have to do something for God; you just have to accept what God has done for you.

Augustine said, "God loves you as if there were nobody else left to love." He is willing to receive and accept you just as you are, if you will receive and accept Him. God wants to save you for more than just eternity. He wants to save you so that He can take up residence in your life.

If you would like to receive Jesus Christ into your life as your Savior and Lord, I would like to suggest a prayer that you can pray to become a Christian and a lifelong follower of Christ. Remember, it's not the words that you pray that are important, it is the attitude of your heart. If you are willing to surrender yourself to the Lord Jesus Christ, get on your knees before God and pray something like this:

> *"Dear God, I know that I am a sinner and that I cannot save myself. Please come into my life, take control of my life, and be my Lord and Savior. I turn away from my old way of living and I want to live for you. I receive and accept your free gift of eternal life by faith in the Lord Jesus Christ. Thank you for answering my prayer and giving me the assurance of my salvation. In Jesus' name, Amen.*

Did you pray that prayer and mean it with all your heart? If so, the Bible teaches that, just now, you became a child of God. You were "born-again" as the Bible says. I want to encourage you to let our ministry know by contacting us with the information below. We will send you some free resources that will help you get started in your newfound walk with Jesus Christ. May God richly bless you as you begin your journey as a lifelong follower of Jesus Christ!

ATTN: Pastor's Office
First Baptist Raytown
10500 East 350 Highway
Raytown, Missouri 64138

Endnotes

1 I'm grateful for the teaching ministry of Randy Pope at Perimeter Church near Atlanta, Georgia. His Biblical teaching on "Facing the Fear of Death" inspired the writing of this chapter.

2 *Tony Evans Book of Illustrations*, pg. 70.

3 Lewis, C. S. (2009-05-28). *The Great Divorce,* p. 75. Harper Collins, Inc. Kindle Edition.

4 Drew Dyck with Christianity Today, *Let My People Laugh* (Nashville: Thomas Nelson, 2009).

5 *Heaven*, by Randy Alcorn, Kindle location 623.

6 *The Glory of Heaven: The Truth about Heaven, Angels and Eternal Life* by John MacArthur, Kindle location 455.

7 Billy Graham, *The Heaven Answer Book* (Nashville: Thomas Nelson, 2012).

8 *Heaven: Your Real Home* by Joni Eareckson Tada, p. 16.

9 http://en.wikipedia.org/wiki/Purgatory

10 Alcorn, Randy (2004-10-01). *Heaven* (Alcorn, Randy) (Kindle Locations 929-932). Tyndale House Publishers. Kindle Edition.

11 MacArthur, John. *The Glory of Heaven: The Truth About Heaven, Angels, and Eternal Life*. Wheaton, IL: Crossway Books, 1996.

12 Ibid. Kindle location 257.

13 Ibid. Kindle location 11597.

14 *The Glory of Heaven: The Truth about Heaven, Angels and Eternal Life* by John MacArthur, Kindle location 493.

15 Burpo, Todd; Sonja Burpo; Colton Burpo (2010-11-02). *Heaven is for Real: A Little Boy's Astounding Story of His Trip to Heaven and Back* (Kindle Locations 1466-1467). Thomas Nelson. Kindle Edition.

[16] *Heaven: Your Real Home* by Joni Eareckson Tada, p. 49.

[17] *Heaven: Your Real Home* by Joni Eareckson Tada, page 22.

[18] *Heaven: Biblical Answers to Common Questions* (booklet) by Randy Alcorn

[19] Walter A. Elwell, *Evangelical Dictionary of Theology: Second Edition* (Grand Rapids, MI: Baker Academic, 2001), 395.

[20] *Out of Your Comfort Zone: Is Your God Too Nice?* By R. T. Kendall

[21] Bailey Smith, *Real Evangelism*. P. 171.

[22] http://banneroftruth.org/us/resources/articles/2005/why-is-hell-seldom-mentioned-from-the-pulpits-today/

[23] http://www.notable-quotes.com/h/hell_quotes_iii.html#C1spTMD2zsP6o2Ph.99

[24] Robert J. Morgan, *Nelson's Complete Book of Stories, Illustrations, and Quotes, electronic ed.* (Nashville: Thomas Nelson Publishers, 2000), 432–433.

[25] James L. Garlow and Keith Wall, *Heaven and the Afterlife* (Grand Rapids, MI: Baker, 2009).

[26] Robert J. Morgan, *Nelson's Complete Book of Stories, Illustrations, and Quotes, electronic ed.* (Nashville: Thomas Nelson Publishers, 2000), 433.

[27] http://www.sermoncentral.com/Illustrations/illustration.asp?illustration_id=8722&rewrite=t

[28] Walter A. Elwell and Barry J. Beitzel, *Baker Encyclopedia of the Bible* (Grand Rapids, MI: Baker Book House, 1988), 1948.

[29] R. C. Sproul, *Essential Truths of the Christian Faith* (Wheaton, IL: Tyndale House, 1992).

[30] Joseph Henry Thayer, *A Greek-English Lexicon of the New Testament: Being Grimm's Wilke's Clavis Novi Testamenti* (New York: Harper & Brothers., 1889), 438.

[31] Johannes P. Louw and Eugene Albert Nida, *Greek-English Lexicon of the New Testament: Based on Semantic Domains* (New York: United Bible Societies, 1996), 303.

[32] http://www.sermoncentral.com/illustrations/sermon-illustration-k-edward-ed-skidmore-quotes-hell-23026.asp

[33] June Hunt, *Biblical Counseling Keys on Hope: The Anchor of Your Soul* (Dallas, TX: Hope For The Heart, 2008), 21.

[34] https://www.youtube.com/watch?v=YFZ1pt0WX5c

[35] Cecil Murphey and Twila Belk, *I Believe in Heaven: Real Stories from the Bible, History and Today* (Ventura, CA: Gospel Light, 2013).

[36] Source: http://thegospelcoalition.org/resources/video/What-should-a-Christian-think-about-reported-near-death-experiences

[37] *Revealing Heaven*, pg. 44

[38] Frederick C. Grant, "Commentary on Mark," in *The Interpreter's Bible,* vol. 7 (Nashville, TN: Abingdon, 1951) p. 886.

[39] Price, John W. (2013-02-19). *Revealing Heaven: The Christian Case for Near-Death Experiences* (p. 47). HarperCollins. Kindle Edition.

[40] Price, John W. (2013-02-19). *Revealing Heaven: The Christian Case for Near-Death Experiences* (p. 80). HarperCollins. Kindle Edition. Quoted Pim van Lommel, "Near-Death Experience in Survivors of Cardiac Arrest," in Lancet, 2001; 358: 2039– 45.

[41] Price, John W. (2013-02-19*). Revealing Heaven: The Christian Case for Near-Death Experiences* (pp. 82-83). HarperCollins. Kindle Edition.

[42] Ibid. 50.

[43] https://www.youtube.com/watch?v=h8W7cD820f0

[44] P.M.H. Atwater - 92 Journal of Near-Death Studies Vol.10, No.3

[45] Light at the End of the Tunnel, *Eternity*, July 1977, p. 15.

[46] http://www.theforbiddenknowledge.com/hardtruth/visions_of_hell.htm (Slight grammatical alterations made.)

[47] http://www.theforbiddenknowledge.com/hardtruth/visions_of_hell.htm

[48] Price, John W. (2013-02-19). *Revealing Heaven: The Christian Case for Near-Death Experiences* (p. 107). Harper-Collins. Kindle Edition.

[49] *My Descent into Death*, by Howard Storm. (Howard was a self-professed Atheist before his encounter.)

[50] http://www.aglimpseofeternity.org

[51] http://www.divinerevelations.info/documents/rawlings/dr_rawlings_near_death_experiences.htm

[52] www.MickeyRobinson.com

[53] Bill Wiese, *23 Minutes in Hell*

[54] http://www.thedailybeast.com/articles/2013/02/08/is-hell-real-people-who-went-there-say-yes.html

[55] https://www.youtube.com/watch?v=GMAKSByShGU

[56] Cecil Murphey and Twila Belk, *I Believe in Heaven: Real Stories from the Bible, History and Today* (Ventura, CA: Gospel Light, 2013).

[57] R.C. Sproul, *Before the Face of God: Book 2: A Daily Guide for Living from the Gospel of Luke*, electronic ed. (Grand Rapids: Baker Book House; Ligonier Ministries, 1993).

[58] Elmer Towns, *Bible Answers for Almost All Your Questions* (Nashville: Thomas Nelson, 2003).

[59] http://www.history.com/topics/ancient-history/the-egyptian-pyramids Accessed April 19, 2014.

[60] Max Lucado, *Live to Make a Difference* (Nashville: Thomas Nelson, 2010).

[61] Michael J. Wilkins, Matthew, *The NIV Application Commentary* (Grand Rapids, MI: Zondervan Publishing House, 2004), 404.

[62] John Piper, *Desiring God* (Sisters, OR: Multnomah Publishers, 2003), 305.

[63] Craig S. Keener, *The IVP Bible Background Commentary: New Testament* (Downers Grove, IL: InterVarsity Press, 1993), 1 Co 9:24–25.

[64] Fee quoted by R. Kent Hughes and Bryan Chapell, *1 & 2 Timothy and Titus: To Guard the Deposit, Preaching the Word* (Wheaton, IL: Crossway Books, 2000), 254.

[65] Clarence Herbert Benson, *Biblical Faith: Doctrines Every Christian Should Know, Biblical Essentials Series* (Wheaton, IL: Crossway Books, 2003), 115.

21107822R00089

Made in the USA
Middletown, DE
18 June 2015